*Pure
Silver*

BY DAVID REID AND

Pure Silver

THE SECOND BEST OF EVERYTHING

JONATHAN JERALD

A Harvest/HBJ Original
Harcourt Brace Jovanovich, Publishers
San Diego   *New York*   *London*

Text copyright © 1988 by David Reid and Jonathan Jerald
Illustrations copyright © 1988 by Everett Peck

Library of Congress Cataloging-in-Publication Data

Reid, David, 1946–
Pure Silver
"A Harvest/HBJ Book."
I. Jerald, Jonathan. II. Title.
AC8.R38   1988   081   87-11900
ISBN 0-15-679960-X   (pbk.)

Designed by Michael Farmer
Printed in the United States of America
First edition
A B C D E F G H I J

Acknowledgments

Right off, we are grateful to Rubin Pfeffer for thinking of the idea for this book, and to Gary Piepenbrink, our editor at Harcourt Brace Jovanovich, for suggesting that we write it. Without Gary's and his associate Giles Townsend's enthusiasm, resourcefulness, and relentlessness it would certainly never have been completed. Gerald Dugan, Chris and Mary Gluck, Ernest Machen, Ben Pesta, and Michael Real we are glad to unmask as coconspirators.

Our parents, Dorothy Jerald and Max and Antonia Reid, were as usual unfailingly enthusiastic and kind. Stephen Reid, aged nine as we write, watched indulgently as afternoons that could have been pleasantly spent at the beach were dutifully wasted on research.

Contents

Contents

Contents

Contents

In life, we end up doing whatever we do second best.

MARCEL PROUST

Preface

Why not the best?—as Jimmy Carter once asked (and did not stay for an answer).

Life may be too short not to travel first class (as Wyndham Lewis said), but it doesn't follow that the entire voyage can or should be spent at the captain's table, wolfing beluga and swilling Louis Roederer Cristal '79. Savvy, connoisseurship, knowingness, and wit are perhaps most visible when the choice is between a California Culbertson Brut (which happens to be superb) or an ordinary French Champagne (which only *might* be). Or between a packaged tour of the Aegean, with a weekend in Mykonos or Corfu (the tourist agent's "best") or a fortnight in Samos (honeymoon choice of the gods).

Too often, conventional wisdom denominates as "best" not only the unreachable but the fatally obvious—an exalted cliché, like the Parthenon or Nathan's hot dogs. If you're still saving up for a voyage on the *QE2*, planning a trip to Scotland just to play a round at St. Andrews, or simply thinking about mixing a martini, there are alternatives you should consider.

The entries that follow, alphabetically arranged, varying in length from squibs to incisive and uncompromising essays, are intended to provoke, divert, and unperplex. They amount to a consumer's guide which is also a miscellany and, in a modest way, a cultural anatomy. Is there an aphrodisiac that really works? What would you put on your toast if all the sturgeon in the world suddenly refused to supply one more ounce of caviar? What is the second best Italian ice cream parlor? Translation of the *Divine Comedy*? Horror movie? Newspaper? Who is the second best political consultant? What is the second best American university? Rock-and-roll album? Single-malt Scotch whiskey? Like what song the sirens sang, these were "puzzling questions, though not beyond all conjecture," and are now answered.

Harcourt Brace Jovanovich's suggestion that we write this book came when we were marooned in graver projects (filming documentaries, deconstructing theories of history), but it appealed to our curiosity and opinionatedness, as we devoutly hope it will inflame yours. Part of the appeal was in finding civilized alternatives (Culbertson, the island of Samos, and Luis Buñuel's martini being three of the more delightful), another part in the opportunity to pounce on arcane facts, to venture strong opinions, and to hierarchize fearlessly. We are glad for the opportunity to discover (or to reconsider) and now to commend to you the London *Financial Times*, the literary claims of the Earl of Oxford, Westbrae's garlic-and-pepper home dills, *The Hasty Heart*, starring Ronald Reagan, Lindt Swiss Dark bars, the zoo on the island of Jersey, Point Sal Beach . . . but read on. The (second) best is yet to come.

JONATHAN JERALD
DAVID REID

Pure
Silver

Adventure Trip

Fly me to the moon

TRAVEL lost much of its zest when falling off the edge of the earth ceased to pose a threat to the adventurer bent on conquering the unknown. Everest has been done. The blank spaces on the maps of South America, Africa, New Guinea, and the polar regions have all been filled in. But if you are truly determined to boldly go where few have gone before (and if you can afford the price of the ticket), there's at least one agency willing to book you on a trip to outer space.

Lest you think this is just another publicity stunt, we must tell you that the founder of Society Expeditions, T. C. Schwartz, is also the man who brought the Orient Express back to life, and whose worldwide voyages to the most exotic and least-traveled locales are now accomplished aboard his very own fleet of luxury liners. Schwartz has managed to persuade NASA to allow him to use one of their launch sites, and a company he helped create, American Spacecraft Corporation, has designed and is building a reusable, single stage, vertical-launch-and-landing space vehicle.

Flights are scheduled to begin in 1992. The eight- to twelve-hour missions will take twenty passengers up into a polar orbit where gourmet meals, designed specifically for consumption in weightless conditions (lots of mousse, we guess), will be served while spectacular sunrises and sunsets illuminate the earth's surface every forty-six minutes. The $50,000-plus ticket includes several days of pre-flight conditioning and post-flight partying. All the scheduled launches are booked through 1994 and, despite the crash of the *Challenger*, not one reservation has been canceled.

For more earthly delights, Society Expeditions offers a thirty-one-day round-the-world tour for you and twenty-three of your friends on a Boeing 727 specially equipped to keep you extremely comfortable and very well fed. The $29,450 ticket includes accommodations in châteaux, palazzos, villas, and castles. Cocktail parties on the Nile, camel races across the dunes of Saudi Arabia, and a trek to the monkey temple of Kathmandu are among the highlights.

These are undoubtedly wonderful trips and must be counted among the best adventures around, the former for its exotic mode of transport and the latter for its global itinerary, but a half a day in zero-g or a month of jet-setting isn't what we mean by adventure. We mean *Raiders of the Lost Ark*/Rudyard Kipling / Hope and Crosby on-the-road kind of adventure. And short of crawling into Steven Spielberg's left frontal lobe, there are few options left to us.

Which brings us to our choice for second best. There are no high-tech thrills on this trip, and no four-star accommodations, but those are sacrifices we gladly make to satisfy our wanderlust.

Just north of the Great Himalaya Range, set within a ring of jagged peaks, lies the Hidden Kingdom of Zangskar. Cultural Expeditions, a division of Mountain Travel, which was originally founded to lead expeditions up the sides of the world's most remote and challenging mountains, will guide you there and provide you with the basic amenities, as well as with an education. Listen to what its brochure says: "In a setting of unbelievable isolation, Zangskar has kept alive an archaic form of Tibetan Buddhism which flourishes in craggy stone fortress monasteries. Along the paths to the monasteries and cliffside villages, there are exquisitely carved *mani* walls and whitewashed *chortens*, evidence of the area's total immersion in Tibetan Buddhist culture.

"This tour includes a strenuous ten-day trek during which we hike from Lahoul over the Shingo La, a 16,400-foot pass into Zangskar. Along the way we visit the monastery of Phuktal, perched on a steep hillside at the mouth of a cave. Within Phuktal's many sequestered rooms are ancient frescoes and wall hangings. Among other monasteries visited are Bardun, atop a rock above the Tsarap River, and Karsha, Zangskar's largest monastery complex, built on a hill overlooking the wide Doda Valley."

We confess to total ignorance on the subject of *chortens* and *mani* carvings, but that strenuous trek over the Shingo La and nights spent camped beneath the blaze of the Himalayan night sky have definitely fired our imagination.

Beasts of burden are provided to relieve you of your backpack, and a lecturer in Tibetan language and literature is your guide. The entire trip takes thirty days and costs around $3,000 (airfare not included).

Cultural Expeditions
1398 Solano Avenue
Albany, California 94706

Society Expeditions
3131 Elliott Avenue, Suite 700
Seattle, Washington 98121

Advertisement (Print)

Beetlemania

Like politics in a banana republic, advertising is always veering between revolution and reaction—that is, between spells of "creativity," wordplay, and image-building (like the 1920s and the 1960s), and stodgier periods dominated by research and "claims advertising" (like the 1950s and 1970s). In the judgment of experts such as David Ogilvy (founder of Ogilvy & Mather and author of *Confessions of an Advertising Man*), British advertising, with its wit and whimsicality, is now the best in the world. But this is a recent development. Up through the sixties, Britons like Ogilvy had to come to New York for advanced study.

A survey conducted a few years ago showed that every day most of us are exposed to over sixteen hundred advertisements, only eighty or so of which are consciously registered. And of these eighty, only *twelve* provoke a response of any kind. (The study was commissioned by the American Association of Advertising Agencies—you'd think they'd have locked it away in a vault at Citibank.) Is it any wonder, then, that there are rich—very rich—rewards for the ability to think up insidiously memorable phrases like "Does she or doesn't she?" "You don't have to be Jewish to love Levy's," and "You deserve a break today," or for creating subconscious-tickling icons like the Marlboro Man and the Jolly Green Giant? Ogilvy, who gave the world the Man in the Hathaway Shirt, is now the proud seigneur of a twelfth-century château in the south of France.

According to a 1945 survey of professionals by *Printers' Ink*, a trade journal, the best advertisement of all time was Theodore MacManus's mini-essay, "The Penalty of Leadership," which appeared only once, in the *Saturday Evening Post* in 1915. The virtuoso of the soft sell, MacManus took indirection to new heights in this effort, which contained no illustrations and never even mentioned the client's name (Cadillac) except at the bottom of the page. Cadillac, you see, had a problem. Its new V-8 engine had an unfortunate tendency to catch on fire, and Packard, then competing for the luxury market, was losing no time in alerting the public to this fact. Disdaining to name either automobile, MacManus took the high ground. (He dictated the whole advertisement to his secretary in a single inspired session.)

"In every field of human endeavor," MacManus declaimed, "he that is first must perpetually live in the white light of publicity. . . . When a man's work becomes a standard for the whole world, it also becomes a target for the shafts of the envious few. There is nothing new in this. It is as old as the world and as old as the human passions," he went on, and just in case you're curious as to exactly what human passions animated Packard, he listed them: "envy, fear, greed, ambition, and the desire to surpass." Fortunately, MacManus reassured his readers, "It all avails not." Requests for reprints poured in, and sales of the combustible Cadillacs jumped. In the 1945 survey this ad was far ahead of its competitors, and if only for its influence, it is our favorite.

A runner-up in the poll, and still legendary among copywriters, was "Somewhere West of Laramie," which automaker Ned Jordan created in the twenties to advertise the Jordan Playboy, a sports car manufactured in Cleveland, Ohio. The headline alluded to the dateline, "Somewhere in France," which had been used in dispatches from the front in the First World War. Below it, a cowboy on horseback rode feverishly across a Wild West landscape, which also featured, surprisingly, a Jordan Playboy automobile. And what was the cowboy looking for, but the sort of woman who would drive a Playboy—"a broncho-busting, steer-roping girl," who had never heard of a number-15 sunscreen. A "lass whose face is brown with the sun when the day is done of revel and romp and reward. She loves the cross of the wild and the tame. There's a savor of links about that car—of laughter and lilt and light—a hint of old loves—and saddle and quirt."

Though this might seem to be directed at a somewhat specialized market, the Playboy did nicely until the Depression cut into the sales of runabouts driven by cowgirls who never got the blues.

We'll give "Laramie" third place. The second best print advertisement, in our judgment and Madison Avenue's, was also for an automobile manufacturer. It was created at Doyle Dane Bernbach by copywriter Julian Koenig, considered a bohemian sort back in the fifties when Madison Avenue was still a sea of gray flannel. (He was reputed to write at the racetrack.) "Think small," the headline advised.

"Ten years ago, the first Volkswagens were imported into the United States. These strange little cars with their beetle shapes were almost unknown. All they had to recommend them was 32 miles to the gallon (regular gas, regular driving), with an aluminum air-cooled rear engine that would go 70 MPH all day without strain, sensible size for a family and a sensible price-tag too. Beetles multiply; so do Volkswagens."

The copy was set in a plain sans serif type with a then uncommon ragged right margin. "I wanted the copy to look Gertrude Steiny," explained Helmut Krone, the agency art director. There was a dinky picture surrounded by lots and lots of white space. In a 1976 poll of professionals conducted by *Advertising Age*, two-thirds of the panel named the Volkswagen advertisement as one of the best they had ever seen. No ad since has broken so much ground so wittily—though not too many have tried.

Airline
(for Service)

The friendliest skies

THE best service an airline can provide is to get you there fast. There's no doubt that British Airways and Air France Concorde services do that best, and they do it in style. Unfortunately, the Concorde has a reputation for starting late, and its destinations are limited (Washington, D.C., and New York to London or Paris and back). While our choice for second best may lack the supersonic zip of the Concorde, the luxuries it offers have become legendary among those seasoned travelers whose itineraries include the exotic locations visited by Singapore Airlines.

When it was founded back in 1972, the corporate managers of Singapore Airlines decided the only way they could compete with the giants of the long-haul routes they planned (Los Angeles to Tokyo, Singapore, Hong Kong, or Taipei, and Europe to similar points east) was to beat them in service. Since adopting that strategy, this enterprising carrier has risen from the fiftieth to the thirteenth largest airline in the world, and small wonder.

Drinks are free, but it's the food that amazes. Singapore Airlines spends more per traveler on meals than any of its competitors. A recent dinner menu for economy class included a choice for main course of duckling in Grand Marnier sauce or tournedos bordelaise, with an unlimited quantity of the appropriate wine followed by cognac for "afters." Choices for business class were lobster thermidor, turkey steak Del Monico, or pork chops bordelaise.

The first-class dinner takes around three hours from start to finish. The elite begin with hot hors d'oeuvres followed by vodka and caviar. Then a salad is tossed fresh on the aisle-cart. This is followed by a soup and the main course, which might be grilled noisette of lamb, venison medallion poivrade, or, for more straightforward appetites, Kobe beef. Vegetables might be rice pilaf, carrots marianne, stir-fried cauliflower, or braised brussels sprouts. A selection of cheeses follows, accompanied by port.

The dessert cart appears after a decent interval, followed by fresh fruit and liqueur. Sound good? There's more. Delicate chocolates are then served with the cognac, Drambuie, Cointreau, and other postprandials, and finally (one might almost say mercifully), coffee and tea.

If you do make plans to fly Singapore, we suggest you deal directly with one of the airline's agents. They are, not surprisingly, incredibly friendly and helpful.

American City to Visit

*The Bronx, and
Coney Island too*

ACCORDING to Rand McNally's annual register, the best is Los Angeles. We'll take Manhattan.

American President

Happy days

In 1948 the Harvard historian
Arthur M. Schlesinger, Sr., had the
bright idea of inviting a panel of his-
torians and political scientists to rate
American presidents. He repeated the
poll in 1962, and one of the most
avid readers of his report, which
appeared in the *New York Times
Magazine*, was President John F.
Kennedy. According to Arthur M.
Schlesinger, Jr.'s, *A Thousand Days*,
Kennedy was particularly tickled to
find that his predecessor, Dwight D.
Eisenhower, rated a middling twenty-
second place, right below Chester
Arthur.

"At first I thought it was too bad
that Ike was in Europe and would
miss the article," Kennedy said, "but

then I decided that some conscientious friend would send him a copy." Sure enough, a few months later Ike waded vigorously into the midterm congressional elections, acting for all the world like a candidate himself. "It is all your father's poll," Kennedy told Arthur, Jr. "Eisenhower has been going along for years, basking in the glow of applause he has always had. Then he saw that poll and realized how he stood before the cold eye of history—way below Truman; even below Hoover. Now he's mad to save his reputation."

Since 1962, similar polls have been conducted by Steve Neale of the *Chicago Tribune* and Professor Robert K. Murray; and for those who still like Ike, we can report that his rating has gone way up (ninth place in the *Tribune*'s 1982 survey, eleventh in Murray's the next year). He now ranks roughly with the "above average" Grover Cleveland. JFK himself is in the same category, on a par with John Quincy Adams.

There has been a bit of shuffling in the "great" and "near great" categories (e.g., Woodrow Wilson, "great" in 1948, is now merely "near great"), but for the most part there is little debate among historians about which presidents rank as the greatest, or in our terms, the best and second best. As you might expect, they're the presidents whose profiles you find on coins—the smaller denominations, that is.

George Washington, Thomas Jefferson, Abraham Lincoln, and Franklin D. Roosevelt compose the American presidential pantheon. If most historians put Washington and Lincoln at the top, in a virtual tie, FDR is only a notch below; indeed many scholars think he ranks with them. As Arthur M. Schlesinger, Jr., has written, he was a "natural president."*

The New Deal made America over, and much of it was in place after

---

*In 1956, when FDR was still a living memory for most adult Americans, the Gallup poll asked, "What three United States presidents do you regard as the greatest?" Sixty-nine percent of the sample ranked him as greatest. Ike, always more popular with the voters than with historians, came in fourth. A year earlier, Gallup asked voters to describe a hypothetical contest between Roosevelt and Eisenhower. The New Dealer beat the general as handily as he had Hoover, Landon, Willkie, and Dewey. In current polls, FDR is still winning.

the whirlwind of Roosevelt's first Hundred Days—from the Emergency Banking Act to the Agricultural Adjustment Administration and the Tennessee Valley Authority. As historian Richard Hofstadter wrote in 1948, "No personality has ever expressed the American popular temper so articulately or with such exclusiveness." The stamp of FDR's quicksilver, empirical temperament was on a whole era. "Take a method and try it," he said. "If it fails, try another. But above all, try something." In 1940 he boldly allowed himself to be "drafted" as a candidate for an unprecedented third term, just in time to become the American warrior king during the greatest war in history. After four successful campaigns for president, in 1944 he was the undisputed champion of American politics. Unless the Twenty-second Amendment is repealed—a most unlikely prospect—no president will ever serve as long.

Of course FDR has always had his detractors. Generations of clubmen grew splenetic at the sound of his name, and a famous *New Yorker* cartoon from the thirties pictured a crowd of affluent suburbanites heading off to the movies "to hiss Roosevelt." In his book *Modern Times* the British historian Paul Johnson portrays him as a basically "frivolous" man, who cold-bloodedly rearranged the fates of whole portions of the earth to satisfy his own grandiose designs. (On the other hand, Johnson has FDR dying in Palm Springs, California, rather than, as in fact, Warm Springs, Georgia—and anybody who can mix up those two towns cannot be considered to be entirely reliable about the American scene.) FDR had a glittering career, but before 1932 very few, outside his immediate circle, thought he was marked for greatness. His tart-tongued cousin Alice Roosevelt (Teddy's daughter) called him "The Featherduster." On the eve of his nomination, Walter Lippmann pronounced him "an amiable man who very much wants to be president, with very few qualifications for the office."

One of the best FDR biographies is James MacGregor Burns's *The Lion and the Fox*. In comparison with Washington's and Lincoln's, Roosevelt's reputation has suffered from a sense that he could be a bit too foxy for American taste. (Not that the other two lacked their wiles.) Supreme Court Justice Oliver Wendell Holmes, Jr., famously described FDR as possessing "a second-class intellect, but a first-rate temperament." Ted Morgan, in his recent biography, disagrees, pointing out that FDR had a fabulous command of fact and, though not bookish (as Theodore Roosevelt and JFK were), possessed a deeper knowledge of American history than most of his immediate predecessors, let alone his successors. (Rather sadly, he was also the last American president to date to have a real reading and speaking knowledge of any foreign language, having learned French and German as a child.) "Make no mistake," the psychologist C. G. Jung said, after meeting him, "he is a force—a man of superior but impenetrable mind, but perfectly ruthless, a highly versatile mind which you cannot foresee."

For the centenary of FDR's birth in 1982, David Brinkley and historian David McCullough interviewed the three living former presidents and the current incumbent on the subject of their great predecessor. Their remarks were all in character. Gerald Ford observed vaguely that FDR was "a good president for the country at that time." Jimmy Carter, who had launched his election drive at Warm Springs and *imitated* the fireside chats, put him "near the top" but preferred Harry Truman. Richard Nixon said he was an "operator," though of course a very great man.

Ronald Reagan celebrated the occasion with an elaborate luncheon at the White House to which he summoned a throng of old New Dealers. (He himself, of course, is an old New Dealer, though now apostatized.) He described his predecessor, whose programs he was trying halfheartedly to dismantle, as "one of history's truly monumental figures" and told how, in Des Moines in 1936, he had seen FDR riding through town in a touring car. "What a wave of affection and enthusiasm swept through that crowd," he said, remembering how he had cheered and cheered.

American University

Veritas

"**I** NOW have the best of both worlds," exulted the thirty-fifth president of the United States in June 1962, arriving in New Haven on graduation day to pick up an honorary doctorate. "A Harvard education and a Yale degree!"

John F. Kennedy (Harvard, '40) would have to reconsider his boast these days. Says Henry Rosovsky, the former dean of Harvard's Faculty of Arts and Sciences, who turned down a bid to become president of Yale: "Berkeley and Harvard are really the only two institutions in the country that have the ambition to be good across the board." In the view of most academics, it's Berkeley that's winning in this elite competition.

In an authoritative 1982 study of 228 universities, conducted by the AAUP (American Association of University Professors), Harvard tied for seventh place in the quality of its graduate humanities departments (following Berkeley, Princeton, Yale, Columbia, Cornell, and Michigan), and ranked third in the social and behavioral sciences (behind Berkeley and Chicago). In mathematics and physical sciences, it tied for fifth, after Berkeley, Cornell, Stanford, and Yale. In the biological sciences, the order was UCLA, Yale, Duke, University of Washington, Wisconsin, and Harvard. In fact, biology was the only category in which Berkeley did *not* come out on top.

Harvard doesn't think otherwise, at least in private. A university officer, guaranteed confidentiality, told the *New York Times* in 1986 that economics, classics, Romance languages, chemistry, biophysics, and mathematics are the pride of the school. History, physics, and philosophy could use rejuvenation, or will soon; while astronomy, geology, English, sociology, and fine arts are relatively undistinguished.

As for undergraduate education, there is a certain amount of truth to the old gibe that the hardest thing about Harvard is getting in. About sixteen percent of a total of 13,400 applicants were accepted in 1986. ("If you have a perfect SAT score, are first in your class and captain of an athletic team, you've got a good shot," says the financial-aid director Jim Miller.) Yale and Princeton may provide more tender loving instruction for undergraduates (as do Bennington, Carleton, Davidson, and Sarah Lawrence, among small private colleges), but Harvard is far more attentive than Berkeley, where undergraduates are cheerfully left to sink or swim in immense survey courses, and the senior faculty are rumored to spend their days and nights waiting for an envelope from the MacArthur Foundation or a call from Stockholm.

Still, Berkeley, which was founded in 1869, enjoys a number of advantages, ponderable and imponderable. To begin with, nobody has ever shot a movie at Berkeley starring Ali McGraw and Ryan O'Neal. As the flagship campus of the immense University of California system, Berkeley shares in the proceeds of a $9.1 billion stock-and-bond portfolio. (Harvard's endowment is a respectable $3.5 billion, by far the largest of any private university.) UC, as of 1986, had begun to divest itself of the stock of corporations doing business in South Africa; Harvard had not. Harvard Yard incarnates every American's idea of what a college should look like, but Berkeley, with its Beaux-Arts-and-brutalist architecture, faces one of the most magnificent views on earth—San Francisco Bay, the Golden Gate, and the Marin headlands. Also, there are more Nobel Prize winners teaching at Berkeley.

Nonetheless, what the *New York Times Magazine* once called the "talismanic prestige" of a Harvard education is solidly rooted. The nation's oldest university, Harvard celebrated its 350th anniversary in 1986. Its alumni, past and present, compose a *Who's Who* of the American ruling class—intellectual as well as political and financial: Cotton Mather, the Adamses (John, John Quincy, Henry), the Roosevelts (Theodore and Franklin D.), T. S. Eliot, Robert Oppenheimer, Ralph Waldo Emerson, Henry David Thoreau, Leonard Bernstein, Walter Lippmann, Oliver Wendell Holmes, Gertrude Stein, Arthur Schlesinger, Louis Agassiz, generations of Kennedys. . . . The list goes on.

The well-founded cliché about admissions to Harvard is that it looks not for well-rounded students, but for well-rounded classes; or as Rosovsky says, "It's an exercise in social engineering." Whether this will lead to such brilliant results as the legendary class of 1910, which included T. S. Eliot, Walter Lippmann, and John Reed, remains to be seen. In the meantime, the faculty superstars include conservative guru Robert Nozick, economist Martin Feldstein (known as "Dr. Gloom"), paleontologist and author Stephen Jay Gould, and historian Bernard Bailyn.

At the graduate level, degrees from Harvard Law, Harvard Business School, Harvard School of Medicine, or the John F. Kennedy School of Government still carry a glittery cachet. HBS, however, is probably second best to Stanford; and the Harvard Law School, which has been torn by the controversy over "critical legal studies," is not as influential as Chicago or as user-friendly as Yale.

As of this writing there are fifty-two Harvard alumni in Congress, four degree-holders in the Cabinet, including Caspar Weinberger, and four more "Harvards" (as LBJ used to call the breed) on the Supreme Court, including William Rehnquist. A recent fund-raising drive brought in $360 million. No other American educational institution is so deeply entrenched in the infrastructure of the American establishment. At 350, Harvard is number two and trying harder.

Anecdote about Hemingway and Fitzgerald

"Dear Ernest: Please lay off me in print"

IN everybody's iconostasis of the Jazz Age, they are Shem and Shaun, Mutt and Jeff, not to mention Rich and Famous—the fabulous gold-dust Siamese twins of American Lit. 101. Paris in the twenties! Suites at the Plaza! Summers in Cannes! "Of course you can change the past!" and "Isn't it pretty to think so?" Scott and Ernest are half the romance—certainly, half the anecdotes—of twentieth-century American writing.

As the one's fortunes rose, the other's declined. By the time Fitzgerald died in 1940 in a rented house off Sunset Boulevard, his books were out of print; Hemingway was headed for the Nobel Prize. But the Fitzgerald revival began within weeks of his death, and as his old friend and rival's posthumous fame grew, Papa sank downward into darkness—alcoholism, madness, suicide. His reputation slipped after his death, and during the 1960s Fitzgerald was probably the more highly regarded, at least among younger readers. On the "Dick Cavett Show," Janis Joplin confided to America that she was Zelda Fitzgerald.

In the 1980s, Hemingway's reputation has been largely restored—it was never lost in Western Europe, Russia, or Latin America, where he is revered as the leading American prose stylist of the century—and together Scott and Ernest are the backbone of the prestigious Scribner's backlist.

"Ernest would always give a helping hand to a man on a ledge a little higher up," Fitzgerald once said, remembering the days when he was the voice of Flaming Youth, and Hemingway was a nobody in a garret. The obverse was true too—Hemingway had a nasty habit of kicking when the other man was down. This tendency put into print what is probably the most famous anecdote about Hemingway and Fitzgerald. It's an aside in the short story "The Snows of Kilimanjaro":

> He remembered poor Scott Fitzgerald and his romantic awe of them ["the very rich"] and how he had started a story once that began, "The very rich are different from you and me." And how someone had said to Scott, yes, they have more money. But that was not humorous to Scott. He thought they were a special glamorous race and when he found they weren't it wrecked him just as much as any other thing that wrecked him.

This was published in August 1936. Fitzgerald, then down and out in Asheville, North Carolina, was not pleased and complained to Hemingway. "Dear Ernest: Please lay off me in print. If I choose to write de profundis sometimes," he added, referring to the essays about his "Crack-Up," published in *Esquire*, "it doesn't mean I want friends praying aloud over my corpse."

Later Fitzgerald wrote of Hemingway to a friend, "He is quite as broken down as I am, but it manifests itself in different ways. His is toward megalomania and mine is toward melancholy." This was perceptive. In an odd footnote to the affair, Maxwell Perkins, the novelists' editor at Scribner's, once confided to a friend that it wasn't Fitzgerald but Hemingway who had been the butt of the famous retort. Perkins, Hemingway, and the literary critic Mary Colum had been at lunch when the novelist abruptly announced that he was "getting to know the rich" (presumably, Fitzgerald's glamorous friends Gerald and Sara Murphy), and it was Colum who quipped that the only difference between the rich and everybody else was that they had more money. However, Fitzgerald would never have disputed Hemingway's right to appropriate somebody else's wit—he knew that talent imitates, but genius steals. (In reprints of "The Snows of Kilimanjaro," "Scott Fitzgerald" was changed to "Julian.")

Hemingway's posthumous memoir, *A Moveable Feast*, contains several spiteful chapters about Fitzgerald, including the account of a comically awful trip to Lyons to pick up Fitzgerald's small Renault, which bad weather had forced Zelda and him to abandon. (The car couldn't be driven in heavy rain because Zelda had had the top cut off; Zelda hated cars with tops.)

There is also the notorious sketch, "A Matter of Measurements," in which Fitzgerald confides that Zelda once told him he was not equipped to satisfy a woman. After a quick inspection in "le water," Hemingway tells him that he is perfectly all right, and for further reassurance drags him off to look at the statues in the Louvre.

"Those statues may not be accurate," Fitzgerald protests.

"They are pretty good," Ernest tells him. "Most people would settle for them."

But really, you should read this one for yourself. The Canadian novelist Morley Callaghan spun a whole book, *That Summer in Paris*, out of the episode in 1928 when Fitzgerald acted as the timekeeper for a boxing match between Hemingway and Callaghan, but "forgot" and let the round go on for four minutes (thirteen in another version), during which Hemingway got clobbered. "All right, Scott. If you want to see me getting the shit knocked out of me, just say so," Hemingway muttered as he stalked to the showers. "Only don't say you made a mistake."

Their last recorded meeting, in Hollywood in 1936, was rather sad, according to Lillian Hellman in her memoir, *An Unfinished Woman*. When Hemingway swept through town collecting money for the Loyalists in Spain, Fitzgerald was in eclipse, struggling to mend his fortunes by writing screenplays for MGM. At Fredric March's house, Hemingway screened a documentary, *The Spanish Earth*, which he had written. Afterward, at the Garden of Allah on Sunset Boulevard, where Dorothy Parker had invited a crowd for nightcaps, Fitzgerald hung reluctantly at the door to her bungalow. "I'm afraid of Ernest, I guess," he supposedly told Hellman. Eventually, he plucked up the courage to go in, but Hellman didn't notice what they said. A few years later, in the twilight of his career, Fitzgerald was amused, or bitter, or both, when *For Whom the Bell Tolls* was selected by the Book-of-the-Month Club. "Do you remember how superior he used to be about mere sales?" he wrote to Zelda in her sanatorium.

In 1951 Hemingway sent a long letter to Arthur Mizener, who was writing *The Far Side of Paradise*, the first full-length biography of Fitzgerald.

"Poor Scott, how he would have loved all this big thing about him now," Hemingway wrote. He remembered a long-ago afternoon in New York. "We were walking down Fifth Avenue and he said, 'If only I could play football again with everything I know about it now.' I suggested that we walk across Fifth through the traffic since he wanted to be a backfield man. But he said I was crazy."

That's the second best anecdote about Ernest Hemingway and Scott Fitzgerald.

Anti-Burglar Device

Hot locks

LIKE Kevin Kline in *The Big Chill*, a lot of us are "dug in": our homes filled with plush consumer durables, accessories of the post-modern Good Life coveted by the less fortunate and less scrupulous members of society. Short of developing an intimate relationship with your neighborhood cop or hiring your own private guard, the best defense against the bad guys is a reliable alarm system.

We recommend a wired perimeter (connected to all doors and windows) with an audible alarm and a monitoring station. In most cases, the alarm will scare off the intruder. But if he (or she) thinks (with some justification) that the neighbors aren't going to pay attention to what might be a malfunctioning alarm, then the monitoring station will notify your local police that something is amiss and, if you don't punch the code that disarms the system, they'll send a patrol car around.

Amway, Heathkit, and Radio Shack all make dependable systems you can install yourself, but we recommend you have an expert put in a system that ties into a monitoring station. The community-relations officer of your local police department should have a list of reliable agencies.

The second best solution is to install a really tough lock. The problem here is that doors aren't necessarily a burglar's favorite method of ingress. Windows and fire escapes are much more popular—even when it's not your own fire escape. In New York City, the likelihood that a top-floor apartment will be burgled is increased fivefold when one of the windows faces a fire escape on a neighboring building.

But let's assume you don't have to worry about fire escapes and your windows are secure. Most doors come with key-in-the-knob locks that present very little challenge to the determined intruder. So you add a replacement interconnected lock that controls both the ordinary latch bolt and a longer deadbolt. This has the advantage of controlling both locks with one knob, to allow for rapid "panic" exits. The deadbolt (it's "dead" because it's not spring-loaded) doesn't just click back if your unwanted visitor picks the lock: the whole cylinder must be turned. But both locks can be drilled or punched out at once. An additional deadbolt gives some added security, and its effectiveness is further enhanced when the striker plate in the door frame is reinforced. Better yet is a vertical-bolt lockset, which features a vertical bolt that slides into steel rings mounted on the jamb. To keep your locks from being punched out, we recommend mounting a metal guard-plate around the lock.

Unfortunately, your burglar may simply place a jack between the sides of the door frame and force them apart an inch or so and not even bother with such old-fashioned niceties as picking the lock (craftsmen just don't have the pride in their work they used to). Or he might use a sledgehammer and come right through the middle. This is why you should reinforce both the door and the frame, in addition to installing one of the high-security locks we recommend.

The best deadbolts are made by Securitech and Schlage. Ideal and Abloy manufacture highly rated vertical-bolt locks, and Medeco makes several particularly tough guarded-rim and mortise locks.

Pure
Silver

Aperitif

For the expatriate in you

THERE is something un-American about aperitifs. Our dictionary may define the aperitif as "a small drink of alcoholic liquor taken to stimulate the appetite before a meal," but we're talking about those exotic, slightly *louche* liquors that wicked Europeans concoct specifically for preprandial indulgence. Our habits on this side of the Atlantic run to extremes. Americans used to drink whisky before dining, or a martini, preferably powder-dry, served up in an umbral bar with red leather banquettes crowded with women of a certain age and men in gray flannel suits. Now, sad to say, our country-people drink Ramlosa in blue bottles or "blush" wines in converted warehouses with neo-expressionist paintings on the wall.

A proper aperitif—a tall glass of persimmon-colored Campari and soda, or a dry Dubonnet—evokes an ambiance of Italian villages at dusk, striped umbrellas, Cinzano ashtrays, and laconic expatriate dialogue by Ernest Hemingway. The alcohol content of true aperitifs, then, is typically somewhere between that of fortified wines, like sherry, and whisky or gin. The ones to get to know hail from Italy and France, where the culture of the sidewalk café has flourished almost since the Roman Empire ceased to be a big success.

Yet so small are the American sales of Campari, Cinzano (dry and sweet), Dubonnet (ditto), and Pimm's Cups, that Campari, probably the best known here, has resorted to low sexual innuendo. Their stylish advertisements let us eavesdrop as worldlings like Candice Bergen describe their "first time"—with the aperitif, that is. In deference to Ms. Bergen, we'll nominate the (relatively) popular and pretty Campari as best. Vox populi and all that.

Second best is Pernod, and that ranking signifies our grudging acknowledgment that it's an acquired taste.

A drink for exquisites only, Pernod (80 proof) is the most famous member of the anise-flavored aperitifs generically known in Europe as *pastis*. Its fame derives from a family resemblance to absinthe. Like absinthe (an elixir of wormwood illegal in the United States), Pernod is clear but turns a decadent milky color when water is added.

To impress your tablemate, add water to the Pernod properly, drop by drop, the way Hemingway heroes do. And be careful with it. As Papa himself warns in *The Sun Also Rises*, "It tastes like licorice and it has a good uplift, but it drops you just as far."

Aphrodisiac

Candy is *dandy*

STARTING in the first century A.D. with "De Materia Medica Libre Quinque" by the Greek army surgeon Dioscorides, it was turnips, cress, and the root of the cyclamen. Homer's Circe recommended mandrake tea. In southeast Europe it was tarragon. The Arabs were fond of ginger and cinnamon. The Romans favored sage, tulip bulbs, snails, and garlic. The Chinese have long vouched for rhinoceros horn. In addition to these, opium, lizards, honey, licorice, jasmine, sparrows' eggs, boiled ghee, sea swallow soup, almonds, and various pepper species have all been considered, at one time or another, to be effective routes to a memorable weekend. Among the more traditional Indian aphrodisiacs is chutney, which, like the clams and oysters praised by maritime societies for their erotic properties, is good enough to eat on its own merits.

The *Kama Sutra* has a number of suggestions, including the use of musk (also recommended in the Koran). Readers of Sax Rohmer will recall how that prescient author, decades before pheromones came into vogue, created the character of Karamaneh, a woman of great beauty and evil, who lured the good Dr. Petrie to Fu Manchu with her scent, which, "like a breath of musk, spoke of the Orient." In fact, olfactory stimulation, in the form of perfume, gets high marks in the biblical "Song of Songs," in the *Arabian Nights*, and in Aristophanes' *Lysistrata* ("These are the things I hope will save us," says Lysistrata as she begins her campaign to head off a war. "These silk robes, perfumes, evening slippers, rouge, and our chiffon blouses"). In more recent times, the relationship between the nasal and genital organs was given at least passing consideration by Sigmund Freud.

To be avoided is the vulgarly popular cantharides, or Spanish fly, so called because it consists of the powdered remains of a variety of blister beetle (*Lytta vesicatoria*) that roams freely throughout the Iberian Peninsula. It is used medicinally as a skin irritant, but there is no evidence to suggest that oral ingestion or application to genital tissue has any aphrodisiac effects. In fact, it can cause painful inflammation. Draw your own conclusions as to how, in less enlightened times, an itching powder could have been considered an amatory incitement.

The best, beyond a doubt, appears in the literature and folklore of dozens of cultures; Shakespeare refers to it in *A Midsummer Night's Dream*:

> Yet mark'd I where the bolt of Cupid fell,
> It fell upon a little western flower,
> Before milk-white, now purple with love's wound,
> And maidens call it Love in Idleness.

Fetch me that flower; the herb I showed thee once,
The juice of it on sleeping eyelids laid
Will make man or woman madly dote
Upon the next live creature that it sees.

Aphrodisiac

This can only be an early reference to what we heard of more recently as Love Potion Number Nine. Unfortunately, the formula is no longer available.

But our recommendation for second best actually has some basis in scientific fact. "Chocolate is rich in a number of chemicals that may have powerful effects on mood," says Michael J. Gitlin, M.D., director of the Affective Disorders Clinic at UCLA. One of those chemicals is theobromine, a stimulant more powerful than caffeine. But the real kick probably comes from phenylethylamine, a close relative of amphetamine that is produced naturally in the brain. Researchers don't know why, but it seems to work better on women than on men. Dr. Gitlin thinks it may have to do with "estrogen's affecting the receptivity to one or more of the chemicals in chocolate."

Along with your chocolate truffles, try a flute of your favorite champagne (see Second Best Champagne). Not only will the alcohol work its usual magic by weakening inhibitions, but those little bubbles will help to hasten the phenylethylamine and theobromine molecules to a receptive welcome in the brain. Ogden Nash was right. Liquor *is* quicker. Just remember though, too much chocolate and/or champagne is not conducive to the object of this exercise.

Artwork in Boulder, Colorado

*Rocky Mountain
high on the hog*

"PIT Bull Rips Voice Out of Talking Pig" was the headline on the AP story datelined August 11, 1986, Boulder, Colorado. "Slick the talking pig, a concrete porker voted Boulder's best artwork, has regained its voice after a mauling by a pit bull terrier.

" 'That pit bull broke from the leash, growling, snarling, and attacked the throat of Slick,' said Don Ray, owner of the Oh, Carolina Pit Barbeque, where the pig has stood since October. The dog struck Thursday night as Slick started talking to a customer leaving the restaurant,' Ray said. 'He completely ripped out the speaker under his throat and it was on the ground, teeth marks and all.' "

Naturally, we read on, our interest not just piqued, but inflamed. Would Slick ever speak again? And—an even more haunting question—if a concrete talking pig is Boulder's best artwork, what could possibly be second best?

On the first count, our suspense was not long-lived. The AP went on to say that Slick's voice-box mechanism was reinstalled, and by dinnertime he was "able to talk faintly." (He is now fully recovered.)

A telephone call to the Boulder Chamber of Commerce rounded out our image of Slick. According to spokesperson Peggy Lamm ("We're all animals around here," she stated gaily), he is pink and weighs 1,500 pounds. There is some doubt as to the validity of the poll which ranked Slick as Boulder's number one artwork, she admits, since it was organized by Mr. Don Ray, the talking pig's owner. Boulder, it seems, has a city ordinance forbidding "talking signs." However, if Slick is determined to be a work of art, the prohibition does not apply. Well, *we* say it's time to end this squabbling and recognize Slick for the cultural treasure he is. He has suffered enough.

But what, then, is the second best artwork in Boulder? "Oh, I don't know," said Ms. Lamm. "The mayor, I guess. Wait! You're not going to put that in your book, are you?"

Bauhaus Architect

"The Silver Prince"

İᴛ was the painter Paul Klee who first dubbed handsome, imperious, cigar-smoking Walter Gropius "The Silver Prince." A former cavalry lieutenant, Gropius founded the Bauhaus in 1919, when Germany was still reeling from its defeat in the First World War, by combining an art academy and a trade school. In its Weimar heyday (the Nazis shut it down in 1933) the Bauhaus became the Western world's most innovative school of art, architecture, crafts, and industrial design. There were workshops in pottery, metalworking, typography, stage design, graphic art, weaving, and stained glass. Wassily Kandinsky, Josef Alpers, and Klee taught painting. Lazlo Moholy-Nagy instructed young photographers. The Bauhausler seized cubism, constructivism, and a congeries of other artistic isms that were floating in the air, and put them on the assembly line, when they were not rearing them to the heavens. From teakettles to skyscrapers, the clean, severe lines they favored have come to define the twentieth-century mise-en-scène.

In Tom Wolfe's riotous, philistine polemic *From Bauhaus to Our House*, Gropius figures as "White God No. 1," referring to the ecstatic reception that he and his associates received when they emigrated to the United States in the thirties. "Such prostrations! Such acts of homage! . . . Within three years the course of American architecture had changed, utterly." Gropius did very well for himself in America, though it is unfortunate that his best-known building is the hulking Pan Am headquarters in Manhattan. In architectural history, however, "White God No. 2"—Ludwig Mies van der Rohe—gets the better reviews.

Mies, who succeeded Gropius as head of the Bauhaus, was an aphorist ("Less is more"), and he said, "My architecture is almost nothing." The Seagram Building in New York, designed in association with Philip Johnson, is the most famous monument of the International Style. "The bronze curtain wall is serene," says Paul Goldberger of the *New York Times*, "the proportions are exquisite, and the detailing is as perfect as that of any postwar skyscraper anywhere." It will survive any amount of postmodernist demythologizing.

Beach

"The most outlandish place in the world"

A THOUSAND miles due east of Kenya in the middle of the Indian Ocean, there is an island with the most beautiful beaches in the world. La Digue, one of the principal islands of the archipelagian republic of the Seychelles, is ringed by vast stretches of bone-white sand, broken only by occasional rock formations that resemble nothing so much as the work of a surrealist sculptor. The blue-blue skies and even bluer sea are an irresistible attraction to photographers and camera crews assigned to suntan lotion accounts. The aroma of cinnamon, one of the Seychelles' primary exports, wafts through the palm trees on the gentle ocean breeze. Best of all, La Digue's isolation means that the beaches are virtually empty.

Diani Beach near Mombasa, Kenya, has also been nominated as the beach of beaches. An enormous reef encloses miles of gentle water that laps peacefully along endless stretches of white sand dotted with palms. In the Caribbean, Grand Cayman presents a seven-mile stretch of sand that is distinctly pink in places (it's composed of ground pink and white coral). Hawaii has Maui and Maui has Kapalua Bay, renowned for relative solitude in that relatively crowded Pacific paradise. And then there is the best body-watching beach in the world: Copacabana beach at Rio de Janeiro. It may be crowded, but it's crowded with the right stuff, including the girl from Ipanema and her friends.

The exotic locations of the best beaches mean they are beyond the grasp of most of us, but it doesn't follow that settling for the closer-by second best means settling for second-rate. It's true that most of California's beaches have long since become crowded daytime discos alfresco, but there is at least one pristine stretch of sand, Point Sal Beach, just twenty miles south of San Luis Obispo but nine long dirt road miles from the highway. The beaches are wild and undeveloped, and visitors can get a true sense of what the Pacific coast must have been like back in the sixteenth century when a Borgia princess offered to fund a mission in "the most outlandish place in the world" and her Jesuit advisers, consulting their maps, informed her, "Dear lady, the most outlandish place in the world is California."

Bedtime Story for Children

A Proustian experience
for Baby Boomers

IN our commonsense point of view, the best bedtime story for children is the one that gets your own particular offspring to go to sleep. Hard-won experience confirms that the literary tastes of three- to eight-year-olds (the prime reading-to years) are wildly various. Some children listen openmouthed and entranced to the epical *Pinocchio*; others, to Maurice Sendak's terrifying *In the Night Kitchen*. Improbably, many children profess to prefer the nightly improvisations of their mother and/or father. The late President Kennedy is said to have related to his wide-eyed Caroline the continuing, vaguely plagiaristic saga of a white whale who dined on socks. Once, on the presidential yacht, *Honey Fitz*, he commanded Franklin D. Roosevelt, Jr., to throw his socks overboard so the whale could devour them. Of course, JFK possessed resources the average parent does not.

For haunting literary and nostalgic power, we nominate as second best *Goodnight Moon* by Margaret Wise Brown, with illustrations by Clement Hurd. Ostensibly written for the very young, *Goodnight Moon* depicts a rabbit child bidding good night to the familiar surroundings of the world, from a pair of kittens to the stars and (of course) the moon outside. The drawings by Hurd are alternately black-and-white and colored, and they include a tiny mouse which is never, in successive panels, in quite the same place. Since 1947, when the book was first published, generations of children have fallen asleep as they puzzle over just where the mouse is. For Baby Boomers (b. 1946 to 1964), reading the enigmatic tale to a child amounts to a Proustian experience. This is the story *we* fell asleep to.

Margaret Brown, who has probably given more pleasure to more readers than Norman Mailer or even Danielle Steel, was born in Brooklyn in 1910 and died in Nice, France, in 1952. She studied at the Brilliantmont School in Lausanne, Switzerland, and graduated from Wellesley in 1928. From 1937 to the mid-fifties, she wrote eight children's books a year, including *The Dead Bird* (1938), *The Little Island* (1946), *The Sleepy Little Lion* (1947), and the cosy and adventurous *The Dog Sailor* (1953).

Beer

This Bud's for you, comrade!

WE know the experts all say there are so many different kinds of beer that it's impossible to single out the best. And there may be some justification for such a defeatist attitude, but this is an area we have explored thoroughly for many years, and if you have your doubts, we suggest you try the beers listed below.

First, if your ideal beer is an ice-cold Bud, don't bother to read any further. We don't like pasteurized beer (which includes most American brands, including Coors), and we don't drink it ice-cold (which destroys the flavor). Close to home, we are fond of Mexico's Bohemia, which undoubtedly has more flavor than most American beers, but it just doesn't measure up to the European competition. For true exoticism, try East Africa's tasty Tusker the next time you're in Nairobi.

But the best beer in the world comes from Czechoslovakia. It is therefore no surprise that the country is highest in per capita consumption of beer (161 quarts per year—the U.S. is thirteenth with just under a hundred quarts). And most of what the Czechs are drinking is Pilsner Urquell, a light (by European standards), slightly bitter brew with a hint of mineral-rich Alpine stream water. A close contender is Germany's Bitburger Pils.

The best dark beer is the English Taddy Porter, which looks like Coca-Cola but tastes like heaven. For a dark beer it's not too sweet nor too malty. Theakston's Old Peculiar Ale is another highly recommendable British brew.

Though they are pasteurized, we have to admit that there are a couple of American beers that, should travel to any point outside the U.S. become impossible, would of necessity be included on this list. These are the so-called steam-brewed beers: San Francisco's Anchor Steam and New York's New Amsterdam Amber Beer. They're not really steam brewed. The term refers to the unusually high temperatures pioneer brewers resorted to, in order to halt fermentation in times when refrigeration was unavailable.

But for second best we return to the source. Budvar, Czechoslovakia, was producing a beer called Budweiser back when the only high in America was from peyote. The only reason we can't list it as best is because it's so difficult to get hold of, and even when you *do* find it, it's the export version (which has been pasteurized). It's similar to Pilsner Urquell, only more flavorful and somehow lighter, which sounds incongruous, but isn't. Its relative scarcity is sufficient reason to include Budvar on your European itinerary. A foaming tankard will run you about twenty cents. *Prosit*!

Bible (Translation)

Good Books

WE refer, of course, to translations of the Bible considered as literature. Of their merits as accurate representations of the Revealed Word, God knows and we do not presume to speak. In due course, doubtless, He will give us His opinion.

The traditional favorites in English are the Protestant King James Version, completed by a group of fifty-four scholars in 1611, and the Catholic Rheims-Douay Version, completed in 1610. Until recent years, Catholic Bibles were based on the Vulgate, i.e., Latin, translation by St. Jerome in the fourth century. According to hagiographical

**Bible
(Translation)**

tradition, Jerome accomplished his task in a cave in Palestine, in the company of many animal friends.

There are lots of other Bibles to choose from, including the Bad Bible (so called because a verse in Acts was deliberately altered), the Bug Bible (a verse in Psalms was rendered "Thou shalt not nede to be afrayed for eny bugges by night"), and the Wicked Bible (which left the "not" out of the Seventh Commandment: "Thou shalt not commit adultery"). Not to mention the more reputable Geneva, Tyndale, Knox, Moffit, Revised Standard, and New English ("Oxbridge") Bibles. The version of the Bible sold as "THE BOOK," and "advertised on television," is not a translation but a paraphrase.

For the sheer majesty of its English, the laurels have traditionally gone to the King James Version, and we find nothing to quarrel with in the accepted opinion that it is the greatest (the only?) work of genius ever produced by a committee. The possibility of divine inspiration aside, King James's group had the advantage of working in the greatest age of English prose—an age bracketed by Shakespeare and Milton, when stately rhythms and long, intricate sentences were meat and drink to its readers. In the electronic global village, translators don't have such luck. So, for example, where the King James Version asks, "What profit hath a man of all his labour which he taketh under the sun? One generation passeth away, and another generation cometh: but the earth abideth for ever," the now-familiar Revised Standard (1952) prosaically inquires: "What does man gain by all the toil at which he toils under the sun? A generation goes, and a generation comes, but the earth remains for ever."

With the proviso that they simply do not have the same magnificence of statement or the age-old resonance of the King James or the Douay versions, we recommend as second best for Protestants the New English Bible, and for Roman Catholics, the 1966 Jerusalem Bible. The latter is actually a translation of translations, being derived from the French Bible de Jerusalem (1961), but is still a magnificent literary work. Both versions represent stupendous feats of erudition and devotion, both draw on vast resources of scholarship unknown in the seventeenth century, and each embodies the decades-long efforts of the leading scholars of its faith.

We confess to preferring the grand style of the older translations, especially the King James, just because it's grand. If the language is sometimes mystifying, that seems entirely appropriate to the conditions in which we find ourselves in this vale of tears. Thus, in the KJV, we are majestically and somewhat obscurely told: "Sufficient unto the day is the evil thereof" a passage the Oxbridge Version renders as "Each day has troubles enough." But that we knew already.

Bicycle

Made in the U.S.A.

NOWHERE is the extended youth of the Y-generation more poignantly profiled than in the evolution of the humble bicycle. No longer is the choice between a Schwinn or Raleigh, three gears or none. Now we have ten- and twelve-speeds, touring bikes, racing bikes, sport bikes, and mountain bikes. Accessories include shoes with adjustable cleats, aerodynamically designed helmets, and clothes that make you look like a member (AWOL) of the Italian national racing team.

The best of the top-of-the-line racers are handcrafted of the lightest, toughest alloys, individually designed to fit your size and weight, and priced accordingly ($1,000 and up). They are made by firms like Masi and Klein. Unless you ride upwards of forty miles a day on hard, smooth surfaces, you don't need one.

Happily, the scramble among European, Japanese, and American manufacturers has produced some surprising bargains that include many of the features of the best for half or even a third of the price. The Torelli Corsa Strada, the Panasonic DX4000, the KHS Classic, the Focus RT560, the Bridgestone T700, and the Peugeot Ventoux (just to name a few) are excellent bikes for the price. But for second best we nominate the born-in-the-U.S.A. Schwinn.

For years, while European and Japanese bikes gained in popularity, most American manufacturers simply imported components, assembled them, slapped on a few stickers, and tried to sell them. As this didn't seem to work too well, they then got serious. Using new alloys—some developed for use by NASA—they began making frames that started looking good to the top riders. Most of the other components were still imported, but the frames—the heart, the core, of any bike—were being produced in quantities that allowed manufacturers to price their bikes at very competitive levels.

The Schwinn Tempo's frame is made from Columbus Tenax chromemoly. The Japanese derailleurs are made by Shimano (one of the best), and the brakes are high-quality Dia-Compes. The whole thing weighs about twenty-two pounds. We say the Tempo is the most bike you can get for the money. The editors of *Bicycle Rider* (who rated it among the top six bikes for novice riders) say it's designed for fun—"like a 6-year-old kid turned loose in Disneyland the day after school lets out." What are all those other bikes designed for, we wonder?

Bottled
Water
(Sparkling)

Drink up from Down Under

"Isn't it just amazing?" we remarked to our friend as we hoisted bottles of Koala Springs Sparkling Australian Natural Mineral Water. "Even as we speak, huge cargo ships are steaming into San Francisco Bay"—we gestured vaguely in the direction of the Golden Gate which, since this was high summer, was invisible in stinging arctic fogs—"so we can drink natural mineral water from the antipodes."

"What is amazing," he replied, "is that when they've been unloaded, the same ships pull out of San Francisco with their holds full of Calistoga water and Crystal Geyser, so the bloody Aussies can drink natural mineral water from California."

In the hierarchy of great American fads, there are still millions who rate mineral water right up there with mood rings and the new celibacy. Many cognoscenti such as Julia Child make a fetish of ordering plain soda water. This, to our mind, is rather like wearing a $19.95 digital watch with an Armani suit—the counterchic is impressive, but, on the whole, we'd still rather be wearing an old Rolex. Or drinking Apollinaris or Ramlossa, a comparatively cheap pleasure.

In this category, we're only rating mineral waters with national or at least broad regional distribution. We're not distinguishing betweeen naturally and, uh, unnaturally carbonated varieties, because we can't tell them apart (unless we cheat and peek at the label). And we're not going into the flavored varieties, because they offend our purist hearts. (However, those made by Perrier aren't bad.)

Topping the venerable European entrants are Ramlossa from Sweden in chic blue bottles, Perrier, Apollinaris ("The Queen of Table Waters," naturally carbonated, from Bad Neuenahr, West Germany), Pelligrino (unnaturally carbonated from near Milan), and Levissima, also unnaturally carbonated and from the Italian Alps. Mexico's entrant (let's have no boorish jokes, *au* Jimmy Carter) is Penafiel, and Australia's, the Koala we were drinking a few paragraphs ago. From God's country, we prefer Calistoga from Northern California and Poland Water from Maine.

Second best is Koala. It's livelier than Perrier, with a nice fizziness and a tangy mineral bite. Also—let's face it, the taste distinctions here are pretty subtle—we're going to give Koala the benefit of the current faddishness of things Australian, ranging from beachware (Stubbies) to Paul Hogan. Koala is the Corona-in-a-long-necked-bottle-with-lime and Absolut-on-the-rocks-in-an-Orrefors-tumbler of mineral waters.

Tied for best, marginally tastier and considerably pricier, are Ramlossa and Pelligrino. The former has a sharper bite but smoother finish; the latter is softer, but a liter of Pelligrino contains as much calcium as a tall glass of milk. *This* is a mineral water.

Buy at Abercrombie & Fitch

A raft for Rough Riders

T HE name is legend. Abercrombie & Fitch, at its original mid-Manhattan address, is where Teddy Roosevelt bought his pith helmets and Ernest Hemingway loaded up on Mannlicher repeating rifles en route to an African safari or a season of gunning down sharks in the Caribbean. (Not very sporting that, shooting fish.) Generations of sportsmen (we're speaking of sexist times) spent more time browsing at Abercrombie & Fitch than they ever did in the Kenyan game preserves.

Unhappily, the original A&F perished in the mid-1970s, but lately the name and the tradition have been revived by Oshman's, the outdoors outfitters. As a result, A&F (twenty-seven stores, with plans to expand to a hundred by 1988) is once more a happy hunting ground for conspicuous consumers with a sharpshooting or survivalist bent.

A corporate spokesman declined to name A&F's "best" buy, let alone its second best—though for "most ostentatious," a branch manager nominates its rhino-hide footstool ($2,000). Good buys under $500 include the "posh picnic kit" ($495, with bone china and sterling silver) and the regulation English-made croquet set ($475). Very nice, but would Teddy and Papa have plunked down *their* American Express cards for this sort of thing?

For most sensible second best, we'll go for the inflatable safari river raft. It's equal to the whitest of white waters, it costs $44.50 (yes, $44.50), and it'll make you feel like a Rough Rider.

Campaign Slogan (Presidential)

"And Tyler too"

Collecting campaign memorabilia, such as buttons, posters, placards, even bumper stickers, has become big business for hobbyists. But, truth to tell, the phrases on those lapel pins and bumper stickers haven't always been particularly memorable. Or, if memorable, not deeply stirring. The Republicans' "I Like Ike," from 1952 and 1956, was merely catchy. The Democrats' "We Back Jack," from 1960, wasn't even catchy, and JFK's official shibboleth, the "New Frontier," didn't really take hold until he was in the White House.

"No Third Term!" were fighting words in 1940, when FDR tried for an unprecedented twelve years at 1600 Pennsylvania Avenue, but nobody's likely to get excited about them today—unless the GOP gets serious about repealing the Twenty-second Amendment and making Ronald Reagan President-for-Life.

Many slogans have turned out to be verbal boomerangs. In 1884 the Reverend S. D. Burchard thought he would be a big help to his preferred candidate, Republican James G. Blaine (known as the "Plumed Knight"), by labeling the Democrats, who were running Grover Cleveland, as the party of "Rum, Romanism, and Rebellion." Alas, he didn't stop to consider that a very large percentage of the American electorate were either Roman Catholics, former Confederates, or fond of rum and other fiery waters. The Democrats promptly seized on his prejudicial, not to mention alliterative, remark and hung it like a noose around Blaine's neck. Cleveland won.

In 1928 Herbert Hoover, the "Great Engineer," promised America "A chicken in every pot, and two cars in every garage." He had scarcely moved into the White House when the stock market collapsed, with the result that by 1932, as cartoonist Rollin Kirby pictured it, there were now two chickens in every garage.

Only a few campaigns, and those not always the most significant as history reckons, produced slogans that have lasted. In 1896 William McKinley promised a "Full Dinner Pail." His opponent, William Jennings Bryan, cried "No Cross of Gold!" Teddy Roosevelt promised a "Square Deal"; his distant cousin FDR, a "New Deal." In 1920 Warren G. Harding offered a "Return to Normalcy," but only because he didn't know that "normalcy" was not (up till then) a word.

"Fifty-four forty or fight!" from Democrat James K. Polk's 1844 campaign is our choice for best slogan, since it is catchy, alliterative, memorable, and made geopolitical history by threatening to inflame Anglo-American relations in the Northwest. (It referred to the latitude that was supposed to separate Oregon Territory from the British possessions in western Canada.)

Sloganeering in presidential campaigns really began on a grand scale in 1840, and here we get to second best. For eight miserable years, the Whig party had to endure the presidency of Andrew Jackson, "Old Hickory," whose humble origins, military exploits, and folksy ways appealed to the young republic. Happily for them, he retired in 1837, and the White House was inherited by dandyish Martin Van Buren (known as "Old Sandy Whiskers"), whose Byzantine politicking and elegant ways were out of tune with the times. The Whigs exhumed William Henry Harrison, an elderly bureaucrat who had been the victor of the Battle of Tippecanoe—an obscure engagement hitherto forgotten about by just about everybody—and marketed him as a log cabin philosopher, the kind of regular guy who preferred simple hard cider to Van Buren's Moët et Chandon. (This campaign was the origin of the tradition that American presidents are, or ought to be, born in log cabins.)

To balance the ticket, the Whigs selected Virginian John Tyler for vice president. Their slogan, chanted at a thousand torchlight parades, was "Tippecanoe and Tyler too!"—our choice for second best presidential campaign slogan because it's catchy, memorable, alliterative, and virtually synonymous with American partisan politics in full-throated roar.

(However, if you were paying attention the day you learned this phrase in your high school history class, you might remember that Harrison, at seventy the oldest elected president until Ronald Reagan, went on to deliver the longest inaugural address in history, catch cold, and die a month later.)

Catch-22

Nothing to wear

In Joseph Heller's *Catch-22*, Captain Yossarian is willing to do just about anything to get out of flying more missions—*dangerous* missions—as a bomber pilot. He's even willing to have himself declared crazy to get a transfer away from the front. But even if a pilot *were* really crazy, the unit medical officer patiently explains to Yossarian, he'd still have to *ask* to be grounded. "And then you can ground him?" No, and therein lies the catch, says Doc Daneeka. "Catch-22. Anyone who wants to get out of combat duty isn't really crazy."

Not surprisingly, the second best Catch-22 is also the product of wartime military regulations, though in this case the rules were real. Our story takes us back to London during the dark, dangerous winter of 1942. The news was ominous. The Philippines had fallen to Japan. Hitler's army was approaching Stalingrad. Montgomery's forces had stalled Rommel at the gates of Cairo, but the outcome of that match was still uncertain. On the bright side, Sicily had fallen and the Allied forces were reported to be pushing slowly north up the Italian peninsula toward Rome. Large numbers of Italian soldiers were defecting to the Allied cause. In order to organize this unexpected bonus of arms and manpower, liaison officers from among the anti-Fascist Italians were appointed and called to England.

Unfortunately, the tangle of military and civil law that governed the Allied military machine and the streets of London wasn't quite up to dealing with the ambiguities created by the presence of friendly Italian officers on British soil. While the fate of the world hung in the balance (and while the Allied forces were desperate to fill the ranks of the fallen), the Italians were trapped in their hotel rooms. One set of regulations could only be interpreted as forbidding the Italians to wear uniforms. The other clearly forbade the wearing of civilian clothes. For a time, indecent exposure seemed the only solution.

It was some weeks before the dilemma was resolved—only the exigencies of world warfare could have prompted so swift a resolution—and the Italians were allowed to join in the fray, fully clothed.

Caviar

Slime chic

SAVVY gourmands favor beluga. Unfortunately, that product of the Caspian Sea sturgeon isn't reliably marketed. The top-quality triple-zero rating is frequently abused, and the contents of jars thus labeled are not necessarily the large, grayish, crisp eggs known to the discerning connoisseur. When beluga isn't available, try sevruga, generally rated just a shade lower than beluga but available for considerably less. Oregon salmon caviar has not yet provoked a salivary response equivalent to that of its Russian counterpart, but in the event of a trade embargo on Soviet goods, it will do.

Now we're going to cheat a little. For second best you might reasonably suppose we're bound to recommend the egg of a piscine species. But the great chefs of France have now widened that definition to include the ova of the lowly gastropod. That's right: snails' eggs.

The story of how *oeufs d'escargot* have become the rage of Gallic gastronomes is a strange one. It starts in Tibet, where a French soldier of fortune, Alain Chatillon (who numbers among previous exploits a search for treasure lost by the Spanish Republican army, as well as a scheme to market computer horoscopes), was exploring a lamasery. He observed devotees placing tiny dishes of snails' eggs (symbolizing eternal life) at the feet of the statues of the gods. Then he watched, not without a touch of queasiness, as the priests gobbled down the offerings.

For a citizen of a nation that regards itself as the center of the culinary universe, this was a challenge that could not be ignored. "It seemed really repulsive," he reported later, "but I understood it was an idea to be examined thoroughly."

He waited until his guide turned to lead the way out. Glancing around to be sure he was unobserved, he picked up one of the tiny cups and tossed the nacreous mass of eggs into his mouth. The stone gods didn't tremble on their pedestals, but M. Chatillon experienced a revelation nonetheless.

On his return home he began immediately to promote his discovery, serving up the new delicacy (which he had patriotically dubbed "French caviar") accompanied by an excellent Bordeaux and hints of aphrodisiac properties. The great chefs were enchanted. So were the proprietors of France's snail farms. Soon Chatillon had arranged for a herd of 40,000 *Helix aspersa* to be made available for the production of snail eggs.

Unfortunately, snails only lay about 3.5 grams of eggs per year (the mighty sturgeon produces twenty). Total snail-egg production in 1986 was a mere 500 kilograms, but by 1989 Chatillon hopes to push that up to a ton. Despite the limited supply and a steadily increasing demand, the cost (6,000 French francs per kilogram) is about the same as for beluga.

How does it taste? Chatillon says the unique savor of snails' eggs "makes one forget the vulgar oily fish taste one often finds in caviar."

But don't rush out to your garden with a spoon in search of new alimentary thrills. Chatillon's snails' eggs are carefully processed before they're packaged. They're rinsed in three separate stages and packed in brine, the recipe for which is a closely guarded secret.

Pure
Silver

Champagne

The day it rained champagne

Aʜ, champagne! Synonymous with celebration and romance, the smug companion of caviar and kings: just thinking about the sound of popping corks or the gentle fizzing of a freshly poured flute conjures up images of revelry and ribaldry. And no wonder—those tiny bubbles of carbon dioxide are absorbed directly into the stomach lining, taking a cluster of alcohol molecules along for the ride and thus hastening these frolicsome hitchhikers in their search, like the Scarecrow's in *The Wizard of Oz*, for a brain.

Two centuries ago, that canny Benedictine monk Dom Pérignon blended the juices of the finest black grapes of the Champagne district of

France and then fermented the mixture (or *cuvée*) not once, but twice, creating an effervescent, if somewhat cloudy, wine. A few decades later, so the legend goes, a young widow of the family Clicquot, turning bereavement into a passion for experimentation, developed the riddling (or *remuage*) technique that gives the finished beverage its clarity and brilliance.

Riddling is a tedious task that begins with shaking each bottle individually to loosen the sediment before placing it, neck downwards, on a rack. The bottles are then given a sixth or an eighth of a turn each day (this is not the most popular job in a winery). Finally, when the yeasty sediment is collected in the neck, the bottles are dipped, upside down, in an icy bath to freeze the mixture of wine and yeasty debris. Now comes the hard part: the corks must be popped to blow out the sediment (the *dégorgement*). A touch of sugary wine is added for sweetness (this is called the *dosage*; the amount added determines the sweetness of the finished product). Then, the bottles are rapidly recorked.

During this process, pressure in the bottles reaches around one hundred pounds per square inch, and before modern temperature-control systems were introduced, there was always the danger of the odd explosion. No one today is more aware of this danger than the proprietors of Culbertson Winery in Fallbrook, California. One warm summer evening in 1982, the refrigeration system at the Culbertson Winery failed and the bottles, not stored in cool caves as they are in Champagne, exploded. All 25,000 of them. That pretty much blew Culbertson out of international competition for a year or so.

Today, the finest champagnes are still from France, but California is catching up fast. (The uppercase *C* is reserved for wines from Champagne.) Picking a single best is a bit difficult. So much depends on individual taste, accompanying foods, and the company in which it is imbibed. Rather let us say the best, in this case, is a collection of superlatives: Louis Roederer's Cristal '79 ($54), a finely bubbled white that has a fruity, crisp style; Veuve Clicquot-Ponsardin's Le Grande

Dame '79 ($50), a rich, yeasty, full-flavored pale yellow white; Taittinger's Comtes de Champagnes Rose '76 ($65), tasting faintly of raspberries with a fruity aroma and a refreshing finish; and Moët et Chandon's Cuvée Dom Pérignon '78 ($55), a pale yellow white with a perfect balance between yeastiness and fruitiness. But Veuve Clicquot, Taittinger, Moët, and Roederer also market nonvintage wines that are generally excellent bargains at less than $20. Nonvintage champagnes are composed of a greater percentage of *cuvées* from different years than vintage labels, but experts often rate them above the vintage labels in blind tastings. We recommend Veuve Clicquot-Ponsardin Yellow Label, Taittinger Brut Reserve, and Louis Roederer Brut.

California champagnes are also doing very well in taste tests. So well, in fact, that the French recently barred California sparkling wines from a tasting the French government hosted for Soviet Premier (and big customer) Mikhail S. Gorbachev. And it probably wasn't just because the French didn't want to offend the Russian palate with the same wine that President Nixon took with him to China for his historic toast with Chou En-lai (Schramsberg Blanc de Blancs).

Our choice for second best is a relatively unknown product of that explosive little winery in Fallbrook: Culbertson Au Naturel '83. It is a deep, full-flavored dry white with a hint of bitterness that makes it a perfect aperitif. It's also the only sparkling white wine in the world recommended as an appropriate accompaniment for tamales. Schramsberg may be better traveled and Iron Horse Blanc de Blanc may have won a few more awards, but the sun and soil of Fallbrook (and the talent of Culbertson's vintner) are producing an excellent rival that has acquired a devoted following among canny oenophiles. And how could you not be charmed by a champagne that, even if only once and briefly, fell on the fields of Fallbrook like rain.

Chocolate Bar

Still looking for
Mr. Goodbar . . .
after all these years

CONNOISSEURSHIP, which used to be a matter of Old Masters and rare vintages, has now reached the candy store. You can pick up a Hershey bar for fifty cents and take a bite of nostalgia, or you can conspicuously consume a Godiva Dark ($3.25 for four bittersweet ounces). The candy counter is one of the few places where all the imports aren't stamped "Made in Japan" (or, these days, "in the Republic of Korea"). If Belgium is the world's chocolate-making capital, Switzerland, the Netherlands, and Italy—*and* San Francisco—aren't far behind, and lately even the humblest convenience store is likely to tuck a few

Lindt Swiss Darks and Tobler Extras among the Heath bars and the Nestlé Crunches.

Chocolate connoisseurs tend to prefer dark, brittle European bittersweet chocolate, but most Americans, as Hershey knows, enjoy the milk chocolate they grew up on. (Milton Hershey introduced the chocolate bar around the time Theodore Roosevelt landed in the White House. Like the cuckoo clock, it was a Swiss invention.)

Second best among the dark chocolates is the Lindt Swiss Dark ($1.45 for three ounces in a handsome old-fashioned wrapper, made in Berne). The Lindt bar, the Milky Way of the Continent, is bracingly bitter, intensely "chocolatey"—connoisseurs refer to "chocolate impact"—and it shears apart with a satisfying snap. The nuttier, sweeter Cailler Cremant, which came in first in our taste tests (a bargain too, at $1.00 for 3.5 ounces) may actually be the less sophisticated treat. (Other contenders in this category are the Suchard Bittra and the Sarotti Halb Bitter.)

Turning to the milk chocolates, our hearts say Hershey's and Nestlé's. A Hershey bar is a part of American life, right up there with the Fourth of July, *The Great Gatsby*, and Ralph Lauren advertisements. But, alas, our taste tests say otherwise and give the nod to Cadbury and Ghirardelli, in that order. Cadbury's are made in the U.S., but the Britons who own the company hew to their native tradition of creamy, milky chocolate with a "cooked" taste. Second best Ghirardelli's are made by roughly the same formula, but the "chocolate impact" is stronger, and the connoisseur might prefer it to the British product for that reason. For decades Ghirardelli's were manufactured in the immense rose-red factory on the Bay that is now one of San Francisco's busiest marketplaces, and that association alone is almost enough to push the Ghirardelli Milk Chocolate into first place.

Cigar

*Where there's smoke,
there's Fidel*

Pre-Castro Cuban cigars continue to be the standard by which the industry judges itself. A musty lot of twenty-eight-year-old second-rate Habanos can still fetch as much as $80 a cigar in public auctions. But *conocedores* (cigar talk for connoisseurs of fine tobacco) say the products of Castro's regime (available abroad or on the black market) are just not up to the pre-revo mark. Not that the Cubans have forgotten how to make a good cigar. On the contrary, the industry still marvels at the construction of Habanos. It's just that the tobacco isn't what it used to be. This is because Castro, searching to replace his embargoed tobacco crop with more salable agricultural products, had many of Cuba's finest tobacco fields replanted with sugar cane in the early sixties. He has since had them planted once again with tobacco, but it will be another five or six years before the soil has recovered sufficiently to produce the first-rate tobacco of earlier times. Perhaps not coincidentally, Fidel is now a nonsmoker.

Of course, there are a few fields that have been continuously planted in tobacco, and these still produce the finest cigars in the world. Too bad you can't tell by reading the label whether these are the cigars you're buying, because odds are you'll be paying $15 to $20 to find out (apart from buying illegally imported goods).

Fortunately, this is a clear-cut case of second best being just as good, and according to some, even better. For when Castro came to power, many cigar manufacturers took their skills—and their tobacco seed—elsewhere. Cuba's loss was Honduras's and the Dominican Republic's gain. Today cigars of these countries come as close as any to echoing the sublimity of the old Habanos.

The Hoyo de Monterrey Excalibur, made in Honduras, is a rich, full-bodied smoke, handmade in the finest Cuban tradition. And at about $2 apiece, a considerable bargain. *Conocedores* will appreciate the fact that Hoyos are bound only with the mellower lower-to-middle leaves of the tobacco plant. Almost as highly rated are the cigars produced in the Dominican Republic by Carlos Fuente, a refugee from Florida. He designs his cigars on the light side to suit the American palate, but infuses them with a blend of Honduran tobacco to give them that licentious hint of Batistan Cuba. Particularly recommended are the Bauza, the Panatella, and the Corona Imperial. Available through your local tobacconist.

Coast

E~AST.~

Cognac

Spirit of the ages

ODDLY enough, it was a tax crisis that connoisseurs of cognac can give thanks to for prompting the creation of the prince of liquors.

It was around the beginning of the seventeenth century, and the vintners of Charente and Charente-Maritime were feeling particularly put out by rising taxes. As if that weren't enough, customers in an increasingly far-flung trading empire were complaining that their wine was deteriorating en route. Actually, it wasn't much good to begin with. It was thin, low in alcohol, and acidic.

Since vintners were taxed by the bottle, no matter what the proof of its contents, and since they couldn't think of a soul who would really miss their wine, they reasoned, "Why not just distill it?" And, by another happy twist of fate, the very same characteristics that make the wine of Cognac (the name derives from the central town of the region) so lousy, are precisely those required for the distillation of the finest of brandies.

Brandy, let us keep in mind, is made from the fermented and distilled juices of fruit. Any fruit will do, but when the word "brandy" appears on a label without the name of the fruit of its origin, then we know (or hope) it is from grapes. The aqua vitae, or eau-de-vie, of thirteenth-century chroniclers was most certainly brandy, for we know that its raw material was wine. Dutch traders who imported it to northern Europe called it *brandewijn*—burnt wine, thus "brandy." Cognac is brandy distilled within a 250,000-acre area in Charente and Charente-Maritime surrounding the town of Cognac.

By the early years of the eighteenth century, many members of the Cognac trading community began to feel uneasy as their profits piled up. For they were, for the most part, British. It was difficult for them to rest easy in the knowledge that their wealth depended on the cooperation of a bunch of French farmers. It made their fortunes perilously insecure. It was time, they thought, to put a hand in. The first to go native was John Martell, who moved to Cognac from the island of Jersey in 1715. He was followed a few decades later by the Irishman Richard Hennessy, and in the final years of the century they were joined by Thomas Hine.

After the founding of these great houses, the manufacturing processes of brandy underwent a number of refinements that have since become fixed in tradition and law. There are ten different white grapes that can legally be used to make cognac, but Ugni Blanc (more commonly known outside Cognac as the St. Emilion) is the most favored. There are six growing regions, defined by climate and soil conditions. Of these, the best are considered to be the Grande Champagne and Petite Champagne districts. (The terms have nothing to do with the famous French sparkling wine; they are simply derivatives of the word *champ*, meaning field.)

French law requires that the first distillation be completed by March 31 of each year, while the wine is still unoxidized. This produces a cloudy spirit that is 28 percent alcohol. The wine is not filtered during this initial distillation, for fear of losing some of the minute, flavor-giving particles. The second distillation (*la bonne chauffe*) yields a colorless, 140-proof spirit. This is then aged in oak casks (the rare wood of the Limousin district is preferred, but because of its scarcity, oak from Tronçais is now used as well), where it acquires a richer flavor and takes on its golden hue. Because new wood imparts flavor more rapidly than that of older casks, the young Cognac usually begins its route to maturity in the freshly cut oak of newer cooperages. As it ages, it is moved into seasoned oak to mature at a more leisurely pace.

During this process, as much as five percent of the cognac evaporates through the pores of the wood. This loss, known locally as "the angel's share," is borne stoically by the local population, which is comforted by the exquisite scent imparted to the atmosphere by the fugitive fumes.

The master blenders then combine cognacs of different ages and regions to produce a variety of commercial products. There are no vintage cognacs any more. But the stars or letters on the labels indicate the age of the youngest spirit in the blend.

The language of cognac labels is the result of centuries of tradition, history, and Napoleonic law. Those quasi-astrological symbols and cryptic initials may seem outlandishly archaic, but there's a good reason for them all. The first star was affixed to labels in the nineteenth century following a particularly bountiful harvest that was marked by the passing of a comet. More good years, and more stars, followed.

The initials *VSOP* do not mean *Versez Sans Oublier Personne*—"Pour without omitting anyone" (though it's nice to think so). They actually date back to the days of British influence. VSOP stands for Very Superior Old Pale ("pale" meaning nothing has been added to darken the cognac); the *E* in VSEP stands for "Extra," and *XO* means "Extraordinarily Old."

Cognac producers have more or less agreed to follow these rules in the language of their labels:

—VS, VSP, or three stars indicate the youngest cognac in the blend is two to five years old.
—VSOP, VSEP, VSO, and VO all mean the youngest cognac is at least four years old and the average age of the blends falls between ten and fifteen years.
—Special names on the labels, such as *Napoleon, XO, Cordon Bleu,* etc., mean the youngest is at least six years old, but generally the average age runs twenty years and up.
—*Age Inconnu* simply means a cognac of great age.

The best cognacs are produced by the great houses of the Cognac region. They are Courvoisier VSOP, Hennessy VSOP, Martell VSOP, and Rémy Martin VSOP. True connoisseurs seek out the fine old cognacs that were once made by smaller houses. These include Jean Danflou Grande Champagne Extra, Croizet Age Inconnu and Madame Gaston Grande Fine Champagne. But be prepared to pay $80 and upwards for these.

Our second best entry is not, in the strictest sense, a cognac at all. It's the result of a joint venture between California's Schramsberg winery (in Napa) and Rémy Martin. It is the first California brandy to be made, as exactly as possible, according to the age-old traditions of Charente and Charente-Maritime. It's the only American brandy made by the finicky alembic method and aged in casks made of Limousin oak. Its name, R & S Vineyards California Alembic Brandy, is both a tribute to the collaborative nature of the enterprise and a sly marketing strategy that seeks to link the California product with the French process. The

Cognac

first public offering in 1985 was widely praised. It is a full, robust, aromatic brandy that stands up well against premium imports. It is priced a little above its French competition, but as production increases, the price is expected to fall. In the next few years, as older blends become available, it should find itself a comfortable niche in the marketplace alongside the finest of California wines.

Cold Remedy

But then again . . .

Two great disappointments of modern medical science are the failure to find a cure for the common cold and the inability of medical researchers to explain exactly why chicken soup works so well in combating cold symptoms. A study conducted by the Harvard Medical School several years ago confirmed the efficacy of chicken soup as a cold remedy without bringing scientists any closer to explaining how it works. An unconfirmed theory concerns the relatively high concentrations of the amino acids arginine and ornithine found in chicken meat, since these are known to encourage the body to increase levels of the growth hormone when taken in pure form and may boost the immune system. But then again, perhaps not.

Researchers in England are testing an interferon nasal spray that sounds promising and should be approved by the FDA before the sun explodes. But then again, maybe not.

Then there is zinc. Sucking on a zinc lozenge (don't try to use the zinc parts of your car battery) is reported to effect dramatic cures. Unfortunately, the zinc cure has yet to be verified by researchers and remains in our file of New Age folk remedies. Our view is, if anything as simple as sucking on zinc could cure a cold, we would have read about it on the front page of the *New York Times*.

Honey, administered by the spoonful, is an old New England recipe that does seem to relieve throat pain. Cold germs can't live in honey, although the reasons for this—again—are not clear.

Our proposal for second best cold remedy was received with considerable skepticism when Nobel laureate Linus Pauling first proposed it some years ago. But since then some research into the benefits of vitamin C has indicated that Linus may have been on the right track. Statistics show that a daily dosage of 2,000 milligrams of ascorbic acid seems to reduce the chance of catching a cold by as much as 10 percent. If you've caught one, the recommended dosage is 5,000 milligrams to start, followed by hourly doses of 100 milligrams. Vitamin C crushed and dissolved in warm water can even help to relieve a sore throat.

Though the scientific community as a whole remains skeptical about Pauling's claims, we do know vitamin C is a mild antibiotic as well as an important collagen catalyst that speeds tissue healing. It is harmless in virtually any dosage except to people suffering from kidney disease. Best of all, it is both safer and cheaper than over-the-counter medications.

Composer
Named
Bach

All in the family

"From the 16th century to the early 19th," says *Grove's*, the German family of Bach "produced musicians of every kind in number beyond parallel: from fiddlers and town musicians to organists, Kantors, court musicians and Kapellmeisters. The greatest among them was of course Johann Sebastian Bach. . . ." Goethe compared his organ music to the harmonies that God might have been listening to before He created the world.

From the miller Veit Bach (d. 1619), whose brothers according to tradition were a jester and a piper and whose son Johannes was the first professional musician in the family, to Johann Sebastian's long-lived but musically superficial grandson Wilhelm Friedrich Ernst Bach (d. 1845), there were seven generations of musical Bachs. They include:

Johannes (1550–1626), founder of the dynasty (three of his compositions survive);

Johannes' sons, Johann (1604–73), town musician at Erfurt (who composed motets and arias) and Heinrich (1615–92), whose works are almost entirely lost;

Johann Ambrosius (1645–95), director of town music at Eisenach, and his sons Johann Christoph (1671–1721) and Johann Sebastian (whom you already know about) and *his* sons (whom we will get to in a minute);

Johann Christoph (1642–1703), Heinrich's son, who composed principally vocal music, including forty-four chorales;

Johann Christoph's son, Johann Nicolaus (1669–1753), who composed organ music;

Johann Michael (1648–94), another son of Heinrich's, who composed vocal and instrumental music.

Then there is the "Jena Bach," Johann Friedrich, and there are the "Meiningen Bachs," Johann Ludwig and Nikolaus Ephraim. But apart from Johann Sebastian himself, the best-known Bach composers are his four sons, known from their residences as the Halle Bach (Wilhelm Friedemann), the Berlin and Hamburg Bach (Carl Philipp Emanuel), the Bückeburg Bach (Johann Christoph Friedrich), and the Milan and London Bach (Johann Christian). C.P.E. Bach was Johann Sebastian's second surviving son, and according to *Grove's* "the most famous and most prolific" of them all.

Instructed in music by his father (his only teacher), the second best Bach spent twenty-eight years as harpsichordist at the court of Frederick the Great, where he accompanied the warrior-king as he played the flute. Bach, who had a sharp tongue, didn't have the temperament

of a courtier and found his duties boring. Eventually, Frederick's enthusiasm for music waned, enabling his harpsichordist to succeed his godfather Telemann as musical director at Hamburg. In *The Bach Family*,
Karl Geiringer describes a portrait of Emanuel from the Hamburg years:

> This elegantly dressed, rather stoutish person is very much a man of
> the world, enjoying the good things in life; the agile hands seem to
> express their owner's caustic wit and his temperamental way of speak-
> ing. The face, however, is full of longing and a poignant sadness.

In his generation, Emanuel was the great man of the family. (The
immensity of Papa Bach's accomplishment was not grasped by the larger
musical public until the romantic era.) He was a keyboard virtuoso
himself and composed over 250 keyboard pieces, mainly for the clavi-
chord but also some of the first great piano sonatas. He wrote the well-
known treatise *The Art of the Clavier*. His works helped to define the
classical style, and the composers who admired and learned from him
include Haydn, Mozart, and the young Beethoven.

Concession
Speech

Vox populi

By general consensus, the top entry in this sad genre belongs to Adlai E. Stevenson, who lost the presidency to Dwight D. Eisenhower in 1952 and again in 1956. Conceding the more tightly run 1952 race, Democrat Stevenson recalled an anecdote told by Abraham Lincoln. He felt, he confessed, like the little boy who stubbed his toe in the dark—"he was too old to cry, but it hurt too much to laugh." The speech was luminous, honest, and funny.

But then, Stevenson—it may have been one reason why he never lived at 1600 Pennsylvania—was a witty man. Congratulated during one campaign for his "way with words," he retorted: "Then we ought to elect Ernest Hemingway."

The second best concession speech was delivered by Representative Morris Udall of Arizona when he bowed out of the Democratic presidential sweepstakes in 1976. His speech was succinct and frank—indeed, full of pith and vinegar.

Primary after Democratic primary, Udall dogged the steps of Jimmy Carter, but never overtook him. After Wisconsin, he threw in the towel. "The people have spoken," he declared. "The bastards!"

Cookware

Testing your metal

Teflon or Silverstone will not do; that nonstick polytetrafluoro-ethylene surface, heated to very high temperatures, might release cancer-causing hydrocarbons. Nor will copper; trace quantities may have nutritional value, but too much is poisonous. And while silicon surfaces have no known harmful effects, they tend to scratch easily, so although they're okay for baking purposes, they're not too practical otherwise.

The best cookware, therefore, has a core of aluminum sandwiched between two layers of stainless steel. Aluminum heats quickly and conducts more efficiently than most other metals. But it needs triple layering to ensure an *even distribution* of heat (solid iron or steel must be at least a quarter of an inch thick to conduct heat as efficiently). Lids should fit tightly and handles should be of oven-proof metal (wooden handles may look nice, but they deteriorate over time and should never go in the oven). Both Farberware and Cuisinart's "Commerical" line are among the best triple-layered cookware, as are Legionware and Masterchef, the preferred cookware of Chez Panisse's chef Paul Bertoli. But for searing and frying, the best thing is still cast-iron, and if you peek into the kitchen at Chez Panisse, you'll see a number of cast-iron frying pans hard at work alongside the Masterchef cookware.

The second best cookware combines some of the advantages of stainless steel and aluminum in a single layer. Calphalon is made by an electrochemical process that actually changes the molecular structure of aluminum, making it harder and tougher than stainless steel. Heat spreads almost as evenly across the bottom as it does in triple-layered cookware and conducts just as efficiently. The cast-iron handles are riveted in place, and the lids fit snugly. Another reason chefs love Calphalon is that the surface is so tough it's almost impossible to chip or scratch with metal spoons or spatulas. It can be cleaned with such abrasive cleansers as Ajax or Comet, which is fortunate because food tends to stick a tiny bit more than on stainless steel. Calphalon markets a wide range of pans, pots, poachers, steamers, and casseroles in a variety of sizes convenient for both the professional and amateur chef. But don't throw away that cast-iron frying pan. There's still nothing better for giving steak that seared finish.

Cruise
Ship

Two weeks before the mast

No longer do fleets of grand transatlantic liners sail the seven seas, ferrying the wealthy and titled in gilded splendor from continent to continent while orchestras play and champagne corks pop. They have been supplanted by jet travel, in particular Concorde jet travel. Now those vast, floating pleasure domes, retired from the mundane job of merely providing transportation, have become destinations in their own right. Among the islands of the Caribbean, the fjords of Norway, the South Seas, and the Mediterranean, the rich and restless (and even the not-so-rich and restless) can relive the good old days.

And some high reliving it is, too. The *Queen Mary* may be beached forever beside the *Spruce Goose* in Long Beach, but the Cunard Line's *QE2*, best of the fleet, is still plying the oceans and dishing out one-third of the planet's supply of beluga caviar along the way. True, the 108-day world trip representing the ultimate cruising experience is a bit on the pricey side (the Queen Elizabeth Suite is yours for about $143,000), but there are lesser suites and shorter voyages. And after all, it doesn't really matter where the *QE2* goes, it's what's happening on board that you're paying for. Aside from the luxurious suites, the casino, the gourmet food, the formal balls, and the discotheque, the *QE2* now sports an extensive computer center and a Golden Door spa. And if you get tired of shuffleboard, you can always try your hand at a little skeet shooting.

Other bests include the intimate, seventy-passenger ships of Norway's Sea Goddess Cruises, which explore infrequently visited ports in Scandinavian and Mediterranean waters; Exploration Cruise Line's *Explorer Starship*, featuring its own landing craft for getting to those out-of-the-way beaches, and, of course, the predictable but plush pleasures of the Princess Line's "love boats."

Our choice for second best, however, lacks many of the amenities featured on the *QE2* and similar ships, and bookings are only available April through August. But it's a voyage which for us, at least, conjures up images from Robert Louis Stevenson and Richard Henry Dana. It's not that we really want to be kidnapped or spend two years before the mast, but there's just something about those tall sailing ships that promises a kind of adventure different from any you'd find in the ballroom or bar of a *QE2*.

The *Sea Cloud* was commissioned more than fifty years ago by financier E. F. Hutton as a token of affection for his wife, cereal heiress Marjorie Merriweather Post, and the 316-foot, four-masted, square-rigged clipper is the last of its kind. The forty cabins may not be as spacious as the luxury suites on the *QE2*, but the genuine oak paneling, antique furnishings, fireplaces, and bathrooms fitted in gold and marble are ample compensation. The corridors are as spacious and plushly carpeted as in the Ritz Hotel, and the food and service are everything a cosseted passenger could expect.

Special Expeditions offers seven summer cruises on the *Sea Cloud*, taking passengers through the archipelagos of Oceania, Indonesia, and the Coral Sea. The voyages last from fourteen to twenty-eight days, and the fare, caviar included, will set you back less than you would pay for a new Japanese subcompact. The current cost of a two-week cruise runs from $4,980.

Cure for a Hangover

*Take six leaves of cabbage
and phone us in the morning*

FITNESS gurus Durk Pearson and Sandy Shaw, authors of *Life Extension*, recommend megadoses of vitamin C, vitamin B-complex laced with L-cysteine, and selenium to prevent and cure the morning after. We'll go with Durk and Sandy's prescription as second best in this category. There are no better cures because there are no *real* cures for a hangover—only the preventive medicine of abstinence or moderation.

In fact, there has been deplorably little progress in this area since Cato the Elder (d. 149 B.C.) prescribed eating six leaves of raw cabbage. You may have heard about the drug Ro 15-1788, an alcohol antidote whose capacity to block and reverse liquor's disinhibiting factors was accidentally discovered by scientists at Hoffmann-La Roche, the pharmaceutical giant. Unfortunately, Ro 15-1788 can do nothing for the morning after, though a dose would put an abrupt end to the night before. (Hoffmann-La Roche says it has ethical objections to selling Ro 15-1788 as a sobering-up agent.)

Home remedies include the time-honored aspirin and fruit juice or mineral water. (Alcohol is a diuretic, as you will have noticed if you *need* to read this chapter, and drunk in excess, leaves the cells screaming for H_2O. For this reason some authorities recommend a mineral supplement to replace lost electrolytes.) Also, caffeine is helpful for those nasty frontal headaches caused by vascular constriction. Ernest Hemingway, who called drink the "giant-killer," used to "cure" his hangovers with a few sets of tennis and a dip in the pool of his Cuban villa. Like many sporting drinkers, he believed you can sweat the alcohol out; and so you can, but only in minute quantities. The relief, if any, is purely psychological.

Hardened drinkers at Harry's Bar in Venice take a nip of poisonously bitter Fernet-Branca. (The Teutonic equivalent is Jagermeister.) If you insist on a hair of the dog, your bartender will likely recommend the traditional Bloody Mary, heavy on the Tabasco and horseradish; a Salty Dog; or perhaps a Ramos Fizz. This should not be a solitary indulgence. Seek out the company of convivial friends, but only those who are sworn not to remind you of a single thing you said or did the night before.

Dante's *Divine Comedy* (Translation)

To hell and back

"**D**ANTE and Shakespeare divide the modern world between them," said T. S. Eliot. "There is no third. . . . Shakespeare gives the greatest width of human passion: Dante the greatest altitude and greatest depth. They complement each other. It is futile to ask which undertook the more difficult job."

Chaucer introduced Dante into English. According to Paget Toynbee's great study, "the first avowed translation" was by the painter Jonathan Richardson in 1719, who did a version of the horrific Ugolino episode in *The Inferno*. The Dante cult that flourished during New England's "Indian Summer" produced Longfellow's line-by-line translation and the prose version by Charles Eliot Norton. Notable among contemporary translations are those by Mark Musa, Allen Mandelbaum, John Ciardi, Louis Biancolli, C. H. Sisson, Geoffrey L. Bickersteth, and Laurence Binyon. Also available are translations by Melville D. Anderson, J. D. Sinclair, and Dorothy Sayers and B. Reynolds, though the last has been superseded in Penguins by Musa's.

Eliot maintained that Dante was "easy to read," even for the reader with little Italian, because of the Florentine's poetic lucidity and the closeness of his Italian to the universal language of Latin, and because he was a "European" rather than a national or local poet. Eliot would lie awake in railroad carriages, or in bed, reciting passages that he didn't perfectly understand. This is no doubt the proper way to go about it. Early in the century, the great Dantista Charles Grandgent used to require his classes at Harvard to translate Dante without benefit of a formal study of Italian, let alone any divagations into literary criticism.

Charles S. Singleton's is the outstanding scholarly edition of Dante in English—three volumes of text, the original Italian (which follows Giorgio Petrocchi's *Edizione Nazionale*), and a prose translation on facing pages, accompanied by three volumes of commentary, one for each *cantica* (*Inferno, Purgatorio, Paradiso*), handsomely printed and published in the Bollingen series by Princeton.

The best literary translation we know is Binyon's, which reproduces in English Dante's *terza rima* or tercet rhyme (*aba, bcb, cdc,* etc.), and is written in a plain but stately and slightly archaicized English. To appeal to weightier authority, it's also a favorite of such expert critics as George Steiner and D. S. Carne-Ross. It appears in the Viking *Portable Dante,* which includes some of Grandgent's notes.

Ciardi's popular version is wonderfully alive, but for overall fidelity, clarity, and adequacy to Dante's immense range, second best is Mandelbaum's translation, which substitutes for *terza rima* what he calls "phonic packing," including rhymes, assonance, and alliteration.

When I had journeyed half of our life's way
I found myself within a shadowed forest,
for I had lost the path that does not stray.

Originally published by the University of California Press, Mandelbaum's version, with the Italian original and superb illustrations by Barry Moser, is the centerpiece of the projected *California Lectura Dantis,* which will include a volume of commentary for each *cantica* and should rival the currently authoritative Princeton edition. Mandelbaum, who is a poet and professor of English and Comparative Literature at the Graduate Center of CUNY, won the National Book Award for his translation of the *Aeneid* in 1973. Hugh Kenner describes Mandelbaum's version as "The English Dante of choice," and that's a blurb we shall quarrel with only to the extent of a word. It's our second choice.

Death

Curtains

Nᴏᴛʜɪɴɢ, it has been (famously) remarked, becomes a person's life more than the leaving of it. Perhaps the death which best exemplifies this statement is that of the great German composer Ludwig van Beethoven. Deaf to the point where he could hear only the lowest of sound frequencies, Beethoven rose from his sickbed to shake his fist defiantly against a thunderstorm raging outside, and then fell back in his bed. No mere mortal ever raged against the dying of the light more eloquently than that. Others, however, have been much less lucky in the manner of their departures.

Two deaths in particular that were humiliatingly accidental, even bizarre, may be said to achieve a photo finish as second best death. Jean-Baptiste Lully, one of the earliest composers of ballet music in France, unintentionally choreographed an extraordinarily graceless exit to cap his stylish career. While conducting a *Te Deum,* he became so carried away by the music that his baton slipped from his fingers, skewering one of his own feet, which was injured so seriously that gangrene set in, and he died ten weeks later. (Could this be the real reason Leopold Stokowski later eschewed the use of that potentially lethal instrument? Who can say.) The dignified Greek tragic dramatist Aeschylus suffered an end more suitable to the irreverent comic playwright Aristophanes. An eagle which had seized a turtle and was looking for a means of smashing its shell mistook the shiny bald pate of Aeschylus for a rock, and dropped the turtle on the tragedian's head. So much for clichés about eagle eyes— not to mention that stuff about nothing so becoming a person's life as the leaving of it.

Dictionary (Unabridged)

Words to the wise

INDISPUTABLY the *biggest* dictionary in English (and the most learned and compendious) is the *Oxford English Dictionary,* familiarly known as the *OED*. It comes in thirteen stout volumes, totaling 16,400 pages; it's an adornment to anybody's library, and it costs $795 plus tax.

Obviously, we're not talking about the work of a day. The editors labored for forty years before they reached the letter *D*, though the pace picked up after that.

In recent years, the *OED* (published by Oxford University Press) has been available in a handsome, boxed two-volume set, which, if you don't mind joining the Book-of-the-Month Club, can be had for as little as $27.95. (The price in bookstores is $175.) Unfortunately, to achieve this miracle of compression Oxford produced a dictionary which can be read comfortably only with the aid of a magnifying glass.

By a nice symmetry, the second best unabridged dictionary in English is Webster's Second—more formally, the second edition of Webster's *New International Dictionary,* published in 1934. It may take some searching to find one, but a used copy should run from $35 to $75.

Obviously, Webster's Second, at fifty-four years of age, is not the place to look for the latest refinements in psychobabble, or definitions of sixties slang, or anything at all related to mainframes, pulsars, supply-side economics, California cuisine, post-structuralism, or heavy metal (as opposed to heavy water). But you know about all that anyway. On the other hand, as art critic Meyer Schapiro once remarked, a dictionary is like a doctor—you consult it to find out what's wrong (or what's right). This is a job Webster's Second performs with incomparable vigor and authority. Unlike its permissive successor, Webster's Third (1961), Webster's Second doesn't hesitate to label usages as "illiterate," "colloquial," or frankly "erroneous." It knows, and so should we all, that to *infer* a fact is quite a different operation from *implying* one, that *disinterested* does not mean *uninterested,* and that fine and valuable shades of meaning separate *deprecating* and *depreciating* someone (and if you're going to do either, shouldn't you really know?). As Dwight Macdonald, a champion of Webster's Second, put it: "A dictionary's job is to *define* words, which means, literally, to set limits to them. . . . If nine-tenths of the citizens of the United States were to use *inviduous,* the one-tenth who clung to *invidious* would still be right, and they would be doing a favor to the majority if they continued to maintain the point." Webster's Second contains nearly 3,000 pages, defines almost a half-million words, and leaves the reader in no doubt as to how each should be used properly.

N.B. If Scrabble is your game, and it's *your* word that's being disputed, use Webster's Third. Heaven knows, anything goes.

Embarrassing Mistake

On the other hand . . .

WHILE serving as secretary of state, William Jennings Bryan invited Switzerland to send its navy to the opening of the Panama Canal.

Second best is an observation by General John Sedgwick (unfortunately his last), made while peering over a palisade during the Battle of Spotsylvania in 1868: "They couldn't hit an elephant at this dist——"

Elizabethan Playwright

Kind Kit Marlowe

SECRET agent, street-fighting man, roaring boy, rumored atheist, alleged early apostle of Gay Lib, Christopher Marlowe (1564–93), the second best Elizabethan playwright, was, to understate the case, a considerably more colorful character than the best—crafty, elusive, hardheaded "Wm Shakspere," who was almost his exact contemporary.

The poet Robert Greene described Marlowe as "mad and scoffing." (Greene's supposed deathbed testament, *The Groatsworth of Wit*, named Shakespeare an "upstart crow.") Thomas Kyd, author of *The Spanish Tragedy* and Marlowe's sometime roommate, said he was "intemperate & of a cruel hart," given to "attempting soden pryvie injuries to men."

Unlike Shakespeare, with his "small Latin and less Greek," Marlowe was a college man, with a B.A. and an M.A. from Cambridge University. He lived fast, and died young in a barroom brawl, arguing over the check, an event that Shakespeare is thought to allude to in *As You Like It:* "a great reckoning in a little roome." Marlowe is apparently one of the few contemporaries whom Shakespeare ever directly quotes: "Dead shepherd, now I find thy saw of might: 'Who ever lov'd that lov'd not at first sight?' " Marlowe was twenty-nine when he was stabbed at Mistress Bull's tavern in Deptford. If Shakespeare had died at this age, nobody but dryasdust scholars would ever have heard of the Swan of Avon, and Stratford would be a candidate for urban renewal. There are cranks who think Marlowe's death was faked and that subsequently he went off to the Continent, where he wrote *Hamlet, King Lear,* and the other dramas conventionally credited to the man from Stratford. (See the entry for second best "Guess as to Who Wrote Shakespeare's Plays.")

Marlowe's major plays are *Tamburlaine the Great,* Parts I and II, *Edward II, The Jew of Malta,* and *The Tragical History of the Life and Death of Dr. Faustus. Tamburlaine,* composed between 1586 and 1588, made him an overnight sensation in theater-mad London. The Scourge of God's arrival on stage in a chariot drawn by two conquered kings was a great *coup de théâtre.* "Marlowe's mighty line" revolutionized English verse drama. Exaggerating, the poet Swinburne declared "He is the greatest discoverer, the most daring and inspired pioneer in all our poetic literature. Before him there was neither genuine blank verse nor a genuine tragedy in our language."

Faustus, in Marlowe's greatest play, is an archetype, the classic overreacher, a perennial graduate student turned necromancer who sells his soul to the devil for "voluptuous living" and the personal services of the demon Mephostophilis. *Doctor Faustus* is an eventful and crowded play. The dramatis personae include Faustus's good and bad angels, the Pope, the anti-pope, the Emperor of Germany, the Seven Deadly Sins, Lucifer and Beelzebub "come from hell in person," Alexander the Great, Helen of Troy, and "devils, cupids, bishops, monks, friars, soldiers, attendants, [and] a piper." But the fatal hour arrives soon enough, and after twenty-four fun-filled though increasingly anxious years, Faustus is torn to pieces by demons and his soul carried off to hell.

> My God, my God, look not so fierce on me.
> Adders and serpents, let me breathe awhile.
> Ugly hell, gape not; come not, Lucifer.
> I'll burn my books. Ah, Mephostophilis!

Faustus has been a popular play from the start. According to a seventeenth-century theatrical tradition, the Devil himself was sometimes spotted attending a matinee.

Encyclopedia

Hail, Columbia!

The "three greatest encyclopedias in the world" are the eleventh edition of the *Encyclopaedia Britannica* in twenty-nine volumes (1910–11), the *Enciclopedia Italiana di Scienze, Lettere ed Arti,* and the *Enciclopedia Universal Ilustrada Europeo-Americana,* known as the "Espasa." This is the judgment of Robert Collison in his authoritative *Encyclopedias: Their History Through the Ages,* and we shall not quarrel with him. The *Brockhaus Enzyklopedie* (Germany's answer to the *Britannica,* first issued between 1796 and 1808), and *Chambers's Encyclopaedia,* published in England, are in the top tier, but not quite up to the standard of the big three.

The lavish *Italiana* is the youngest

and most beautiful of the great national encyclopedias, a masterpiece of design from the world's most intensely visual culture. It was published in thirty-six volumes during the years 1929–39 under the editorship of Giovanni Gentile. Gentile was known as the philosopher of fascism, but the encyclopedia, which is otherwise impartial, survived Mussolini's fall. Appendices have since appeared at (roughly) twelve-year intervals.

The "Espasa" was the longest in the making, published in Barcelona in seventy-one volumes from 1905 to 1930, and is still the biggest in print. Like the *Italiana,* it's been updated in periodic supplements, rather than being continuously revised, as is the *Britannica.* A ten-volume supplement was issued almost as soon as it was completed, and there is a *Suplemento anual,* which, however, is generally *not* published annually. The "Espasa" is intricately detailed ("maps and plans of even remote and obscure places") and includes a dictionary, like the French *Grand Larousse Encyclopédique.*

Like gunpowder and movable type, encyclopedias have two distinct histories, one in the West, another in China. (There were also important Arab encyclopedias, beginning at the time of our Middle Ages.) The most notable classical encyclopedia was a miscellany by Pliny the Elder (the oldest such proto-encyclopedia was compiled around 370 B.C.). Chinese encyclopedias, appearing around the third century A.D., were gigantic affairs, sometimes centuries in completion, often running for hundreds of volumes and (by Western standards) eccentrically organized. The great Argentine writer Jorge Luis Borges claimed to have seen a "certain Chinese encyclopedia" in which the category *animals* was broken into such subsections as "belonging to the emperor," "suckling pigs," "sirens," and "from a long way off look like flies."

The biggest Western encyclopedia was the unfinished *Allgemeine Encyclopädie* in 167 volumes, including a famous 3,668-page entry on Greece. Historically, the most significant was Diderot's scientific and skeptical *Encyclopédie,* which heated up the political climate just in time for the French Revolution. Both of these encyclopedias organized knowledge by way of the topical treatise, a throwback to medieval summas, rather than by detailed particular entry. A great might-have-been in the same category is the *Encyclopedia Metropolitana,* which was proposed in the early nineteenth century. By then, unfortunately, buyers shied away from an encyclopedia that was to be organized systematically (after a scheme devised by Samuel Taylor Coleridge), rather than alphabetically.

The eleventh edition of the *Britannica* contains many of the masterly articles written for the ninth edition, hitherto its best, including contributions by T. H. Huxley, George Saintsbury, Swinburne, J. A. Symonds, John Morley, Lord Macaulay, and William Morris, with new entries by Baron von Hugel, Lister, the physicist Rutherford, and others. Editorial supervision and coordination were tighter than ever before, and for the first time, nothing went to press until the whole was completed. It was printed on durable India paper. If you find an original edition, our advice is to say you'll take it. Period. Inquire as to price afterward.

Less famous, but in some ways an even better buy, is the thirteenth edition, completed after the First World War. It reprints the eleventh edition, with the addition of three supplemental volumes including entries by Albert Einstein ("Space-Time"), Freud ("Psycho-analysis"), and Henry Ford ("Mass Production").

As Collison points out, it is a myth that encyclopedias are ever superseded; "rather, an older edition may well include more detail and better balanced information on such subjects, for encyclopaedias are very much slaves of fashion and, in order to insert an article on POP MUSIC, they will cheerfully chop off one of the paragraphs of an article on Alexander Pope."

The *Britannica* is still the outstanding reference work in English— though for various reasons including the (much exaggerated) knowledge "explosion," the decline in the number of scholars who know how to write, and diminished expectations among publishers of their audiences, none of the recent editions is comparable to the eleventh in literary force or general authoritativeness.

Anglophiles will note that the eleventh was the last edition to be written mainly in England. Shortly afterward, its copyright was transferred to the U.S., where *Britannica* fell among the Aristotelians of the University of Chicago. In 1974, after decades of so-called "continuous revision," the *Britannica* appeared in an entirely new thirty-volume arrangement, including the *Propaedia,* a one-volume outline; the *Micropaedia,* ten volumes of short entries; and the *Macropaedia,* in nineteen volumes. For years, it seemed, not a copy of *TV Guide* was published without showing Lucille Ball exulting over the cumbersome arrangement.

Though we deplore this hybrid, we admit the current *Britannica* is still the best encyclopedia in English in print. The popular *Encyclopaedia Americana,* continuously revised since 1911, is strong on American topics and includes summaries of major works of literature and music. Like the more scholarly *Chambers's,* it's a worthy enough alternative, at least since the *Britannica* adopted its inside-out format.

Second best is a solid desk encyclopedia in one volume. In this category, tops is *The New Columbia Encyclopedia,* published by Columbia University Press in 1975. For the working writer and the reasonably diligent collegian, the *NCE* is as a indispensable as desk dictionary, almanac, and thesaurus. If your thirst for knowledge about Tiglath-pileser III ("d. 728 B.C., king of ancient Assyria"), the Thomson effect, or Roger Taney is unquenchable, you can always check out the reference room of a good library. But if you simply *need* to know—in a hurry—what a Tiglath-pileser, or a Thomson effect, or a Roger Taney *is,* the *New Columbia* will tell you. " 'First aid and essential facts' rather than technical treatises," as Collison says.

Columbia's first edition was published in 1935. Its editor, Clarke Fisher Ansley, said charmingly that his aim was an encyclopedia compact and simple enough to guide the "young Abraham Lincoln." Collison describes the work as "a very scholarly attempt to bridge the gap between the large learned encyclopedias and the cheap popular works; though it is compact it is comprehensive for, by omitting definitions, more space has been made available for essentially encyclopedic information. Cross-references are plentiful, thus eliminating the need for repeating information. . . ." There are charts of constellations, popes, and presidents, and entries for every proper name in the King James Bible.

The *Columbia* is a second best that's also a best buy. For as little as $35 on sale, you get 28,000 entries, from *A* ("a letter of the alphabet") to *Zyrians* ("see KOWI": that sounds like Borges, doesn't it?). That is as much learning as you're going to get for as little money.

English Poet Who Died Young

"Sleepless Soul"

NOTABLE English poets who died before their thirty-first birthdays include the sonneteer Henry Howard, Earl of Surrey (executed for treason at twenty-nine), Christopher Marlowe (killed in a barroom brawl at the same age), and Emily Brontë, the author of *Wuthering Heights* (died of tuberculosis, aged thirty).

The romantic poets were famous for dying young. However, you're not going to catch *us* weighing the competing claims of John Keats (1795–1821) or Percy Bysshe Shelley (1792–1822). Or even pausing to consider whether Byron, dead at thirty-six, died young. We shall simply leave these top bards in peace on Parnassus, and on sentimental grounds nominate as second best the romantics' own favorite poet-who-died-young—Thomas Chatterton (d. 1770), forger and fabulist, who tore up his manuscripts and swallowed arsenic in a furnished room in London, at the age of seventeen.

In love with the medieval past, Chatterton was mediocre when writing in his own persona, but capable of genius as "Thomas Rowley," the fifteenth-century priest whose manuscripts he claimed to have discovered. Samuel Johnson, who easily detected the fakes, nonetheless described Chatterton as "the most extraordinary young man that has encountered my knowledge. It is wonderful how the whelp has written such things." In "Resolution and Independence," Wordsworth memorializes him as "the marvelous Boy, / The sleepless Soul who perished in his pride."

English University

"The Other Place"

THERE were forty-two universities in Great Britain the last time we counted—but the other forty, collectively, do not command the prestige that the two oldest, Oxford and Cambridge, can claim individually. Founded in the twelfth century, Oxford and Cambridge were world-famous when the other great European centers of learning were Salamanca, Prague, Bologna, and Constantinople. They still somewhat overshadow such comparatively raw campuses as Berkeley and Harvard (America's best and second best). For academic Anglophiles they are the holy of holies.

Both universities contain a congeries of individual colleges (Oxford's are more autonomous), and instruction in both is based on the tutorial, as opposed to the lecture system of the Continent and the United States. However, as Noel Annan (a Cantabrigian) points out, "Although the ancient universities resemble each other more than they do any other university, their alumni love to depict the subtle distinctions which evoke in Cambridge an ethos different from that of Oxford." Thus, he says, Oxford is supposed to be worldly, Cambridge otherworldly. Architecturally, Oxford is grand, Cambridge "barer, more austere." At Oxford, philosophy is still Queen of the Sciences; Cambridge grubs in laboratories. The neutron was discovered at Cambridge, and at Cambridge's Cavendish Laboratory, Watson and Crick cracked the genetic code and discovered the double helix. Oxford produced Newman and the Oxford Movement; Cambridge, Hallam, Tennyson, and the "Apostles." It is also clearly superior in hatching spy rings (Kim Philby is an alumnus).

We give the nod to Oxford as best, in deference to its slightly greater antiquity (Cambridge was founded by some clerks of Oxenford who migrated when townies took to lynching students), to its devotion to the humanities unbroken since the Middle Ages, and to the fact that it has produced more great statesmen and perhaps as many great thinkers. (Not so many great poets, however. Wordsworth, Byron, and Tennyson, among others, were Cambridge men. Byron kept a bear in his rooms.)

Also, there are more recorded anecdotes about Oxford, perhaps because of the self-regard that has led Oxford University Press to issue an *Oxford Book of Oxford*. Many of these stories concern town-and-gown relations, or the asperity or unworldliness of dons. Balliol, perhaps the grandest Oxford college, has inspired a disproportionate number of these stories. We particularly like the one about the Master of Balliol who attempted to quiet an enraged mob with a speech that began, "My deluded friends . . ." A successor of his was the classicist Benjamin Jowett. It is said that Jowett, after listening to a new poem by the then poet laureate, remarked, "I think I wouldn't publish that, if I were you, Tennyson." "Well, if it comes to that, Master," Tennyson replied, "the sherry you gave us at luncheon was beastly."

As opposed to Oxford's flamboyance, says Annan, "Impersonality, lack of excess, *nil admirari* are said to be Cambridge characteristics, the tone of voice less playful, witty and *mondain,* the dry biscuit served with the Oxford Madeira." Cambridge shaped, and has been shaped by, the scientific ethos. Isaac Newton studied and taught at Cambridge, as did Maxwell, Rutherford, and Thomson. Bertrand Russell and A. N. Whitehead produced their epoch-making *Principia Mathematica* at Cambridge. King's College was home to the economist Lord Keynes, and also to novelist E. M. Forster, a fellow aesthete and "Bloomsberry."

Cambridge's colleges include Peterhouse (founded 1284), Clare (1326), Magdalene (1542), and Trinity (1546). In case you're wondering, "The Other Place" was, at one time, Oxford's preferred designation for the colleges on the Cam.

Espresso Maker

Mohammed's cup

PART of the mystique of espresso lies in the functional beauty of the machinery required to brew it. No café in France or Italy would be complete without one of those gleaming contraptions consecrated to the Age of Steam. But although those knobs and levers hint at mysterious and complex alchemical functions, essentially they perform a simple operation. Whether the espresso maker employs a hydraulic or spring-powered piston, the process is the same. A small quantity of hot water is forced under pressure through tightly packed coffee grounds, producing a thick dribble of black liquid—ready to serve with a thin slice of lemon peel or, as cappuccino, with foamed milk.

One great advantage of the espresso system is the speed with which it operates. The longer the grounds remain in contact with hot water, the more bitter-tasting ingredients are also extracted. In the espresso process the pressurized water is forced so rapidly through the grounds that it draws out only the most mellow and pleasant-tasting solutes.

The first espresso machine, invented by Louis Bernard Rabaut in 1822, operated on the same principles still employed by many commercial machines and most home systems today. A large, pressurized reservoir filled with hot water is connected through a system of valves to a filter trap containing tightly packed grounds. When the primary valve is opened, hot water is forced through the trap. The problem with Rabaut's invention was that it required constant attention to maintain an even pressure. The solution was to increase the number of valves between the reservoir and the filter, creating an appearance which suggested the boiler room of a steamship. Sometime during the 1920s, levers were added to the café machines. These were attached to a piston above a smaller reservoir above the trap. When the hot water filled the reservoir, the operator pulled down the handle, forcing the water through the grounds. But here again consistency was dependent upon the speed and force of the human operator. The introduction of a spring-loaded piston helped somewhat, but it wasn't until the sixties that the latest refinement was introduced.

The newest generation of espresso machines is once again lever-less, utilizing instead a hydraulic piston that sits above the small reservoir. When that is full, a valve automatically opens, and tap water forces the piston down, always with the same speed and pressure, producing, at last, a consistent result—though without the theatrical flourish of the hand-driven lever.

The sheer size of the commercial machines gives them one great advantage over home machines. They produce more pressure and therefore deliver a better-tasting result. The best, if you can afford them, are made by Gaggia and are available at restaurant-supply outfits.

If you want something less imposing and expensive, there are a number of home machines available that come close to the commercial colossi. The best of these is undoubtedly the Krups-Gaggia, which operates on the push-button, hydraulic piston principle and consistently produces an excellent result. The Olympia Maxi-Matic and the Riviera are also highly rated, but are equally expensive.

For second best, we recommend the Olympia Cremina. It costs considerably less than those listed above and, if operated carefully, makes an equally satisfying espresso. Best of all, it is lever driven (which means there are fewer things that can go wrong), and it's fun and impressive to operate. It also has the largest water capacity of any of the home machines—four quarts.

Just keep in mind that the average demitasse of espresso contains up to 200 milligrams of caffeine (that's twice the amount in a whole cup of American coffee), and should therefore be consumed with due respect for its effects. According to a Persian tale, these were long ago recognized by the prophet Mohammed, who was served his first cup by the angel Gabriel. Mohammed reported with both approval and caution that he "felt able to unseat forty horsemen and possess fifty women."

Etiquette Book

Excruciatingly correct

THE popularity of books of etiquette is a cyclical phenomenon, like sunspots or short skirts. The demand is typically greatest when a lot of people are either getting rich, or expect to get rich, or at least look forward to a nice promotion and attendant nerve-wracking dinners at the boss's house or, more nerve-wracking, dinners for the boss at their house (condo, apartment).

That said, we think the second best book of etiquette for the purposes of today's would-be well-mannered is not by Emily Post, or Amy Vanderbilt, or any of the other aristocratic ladies in slightly reduced circumstances who used to monopolize the market (almost as bad as monopolizing the conversation). The second best book of etiquette (and a considerable two-for-the-price-of-one bargain) is *Miss Manners' Guide to Rearing Perfect Children.* It's runner-up to *Miss Manners' Guide to Excruciatingly Correct Behavior,* a wonderfully comprehensive book that is unmatched for authoritative good sense. If you'll just hold still for a moment (stop squirming! sit up straight!), we'll tell you why *Rearing Perfect Children* may be the better buy, even if you are not now contemplating making your own personal addition to the latest baby boom.

Even the earlier editions of Emily Post's *Etiquette,* originally published in 1922, and the best guide until Miss Manners arrived on the scene, belong to a world as exotic as Byzantium, and in some respects as over-refined. In fact, as Edmund Wilson discovered, they amount to a kind of medieval allegory, featuring characters like Bobo Gildings (one of the Gildings of Golden Hall), the Worldlies of Great Estates, the Toplofties, the Gailys (not what you think), poor little Miss Nobackground, awful Mr. Richan Vulgar, and the unspeakable "Guest No One Invites Again." Their world has its agreeable aspects. One imagines a lot of pouring of martinis from chromium-and-glass shakers, and everybody can afford at least a maid.

In *Rearing Perfect Children,* Miss Manners has to wrestle with questions that Emily Post would have considered it a breach of etiquette even to think about, e.g., what to do when conjugal visits by the "good friends" of divorced mommies and daddies are invaded by nosy offspring. ("Miss Manners is reluctant to acknowledge that any etiquette situation is hopeless, but this one is close.") Or bathroom behavior. ("In vain does Miss Manners cry that she doesn't care what people do in the bathroom—she doesn't want to think about it—if only they will shut the door first.")

As a guide to the mysteries of how to eat an artichoke (with your fingers, very carefully), how to dress a wedding party, write a bread-and-butter note, or address the president (no matter what you think of his policy in Central America), the encyclopedic *Guide to Excruciatingly Correct Behavior* is unlikely to be supplanted for a great many years. What makes the second best *Guide to Rearing Perfect Children* such a superb buy is that it covers the essentials for adults as well as the even more labyrinthine mysteries announced by its title.

On the "Great Fork Debate": "Use the one farthest to the left. That's all there is to know. The knives follow along in kind, from the outside in, one knife and fork per course. If you do use the wrong fork (an event that happens far less often than Miss Manners' mail would suggest), lick it clean and slip it back onto the tablecloth when no one is looking."

On "Restaurant Rights": "Remain ignorant of the personnel hierarchy of the restaurant. If a restaurant employs an army of captains, waiters, headwaiters, priests of wine, busboys, and hostesses, that is its privilege. But the customer should not be expected to recognize and treat according to rank the entire service. . . . One would think that if the people sitting at one's restaurant table are satisfied with one's manners, one would hardly care about the opinion of those standing behind it."

On names: "Up to the age of seventeen, children are allowed free play with their names, even to the point of changing names that end in *y* to *i*, which of course they all do anyway. Upon leaving high school, they must each pick a permanent first name. On beginning college or employment, they must tell everyone the new name, pretending they have always had it, but they are not allowed to chastise relations and childhood friends for using the old one."

On the larger subject of rearing children, Miss Manners takes the view that the "chief tools" must be "example and nagging." She does not believe children are born preferring Big Macs to all other foods. And she has straightforward preppie tastes in determining how they should be dressed (no "Judas Priest" T-shirts). She thinks children should be taught to write thank-you notes as soon as they graduate from crayons, though she was somewhat taken aback by the correspondent who wanted to determine the "proper use of hand-lettered calling cards for little girls and boys." ("Little boys and girls do not properly have calling cards," she replied severely, "not even if they are in the habit of paying formal morning calls or sending flowers to their hostesses, the chief uses of such cards.") Her survey takes her from the nursery to "Adult Romance (More Things Mother Never Mentioned)"; she is always tart and sensible, often witty, occasionally epigrammatic—as in "Rules for Roommates" (about collegiate life), which declares, "Virtue should have some rewards. Roommates are not generally among them." Or: "That people will do anything to please their children is evident from the number of people who explain that they are getting divorced for their sake."

Her publisher identifies Miss Manners as "a registered trademark," which makes one fear some long-term plot to turn her into a mere brand-name dispenser of advice on the order of Betty Crocker. The real, irreplaceable Miss Manners is Judith Martin, who writes a column on etiquette for the *Washington Post,* from which her books have been compiled, and who has lectured on the subject at Harvard University (published in book form in 1985 under the title *Common Courtesy*). Emily Post thought it was her mission in life to show the world how the "Best People" behaved so that the rest of us could follow warily in their footsteps; modest Miss Manners describes herself as a student of "folk customs."

In this spirit, and for occasions when all else fails, she provides "A Glossary of Parental Expressions, Traditional and Useful," including (her capital letters) "BECAUSE," "BUT HE'S SUCH A NICE BOY (Admonition to daughter meaning 'We like his parents')," "GO PUT ON A SWEATER," "WE'RE NOT MADE OF MONEY," "TOO BAD, YOU GOT THE ONLY ROTTEN PARENTS ON THE BLOCK (Alternative, with snobby overtones: 'Well, we're not everybody else')," and the classic "YOU'LL UNDERSTAND WHEN YOU HAVE CHILDREN." The last is correctly described as an "all-purpose retort, the truth of which is proven in that no child understands it, but all parents use it."

Female Mad Scene in Opera

Dames at Sea

ODDLY, there are few great *male* mad scenes in opera, the best being that of Modest Mussorgsky's *Boris Godunov,* a spine-tingling affair complete with hallucinations, a toppled throne, and the obligatory roll down a steep flight of stairs—a favorite of black-and-blue bassos who pine to be the next Chaliapin. But there are literally dozens of female mad scenes in nineteenth-century Italian opera, most of them inspired by a romantic adoration for Ophelia's demented histrionics in Shakespeare's *Hamlet*—a favorite play of the era. Ambroise Thomas pulled off a moderately entertaining version of Ophelia's antics in his opera *Hamlet.* But it is generally conceded that nothing can compete with the all-stops-pulled coloratura fireworks of the mad scene of Gaetano Donizetti's *Lucia di Lammermoor,* adapted from the Walter Scott novel. Having stabbed and murdered the husband her brother has foisted upon her, the blood-stained Lucia warbles prettily for a good twenty minutes (at one point echoing the notes of a flute which only she, in true Keatsian manner, can hear), all the while essaying incredibly difficult trills and roulades before the obligatory climactic E-flat *in alt*—the inevitable cue for her abrupt expiration before her horrified wedding guests. This role was the province of canary-bird soubrettes until the 1950s, when *La Divina* herself, the great Maria Callas, restored it to its full grandeur by portraying Lucia as authentically, horrifyingly insane. This portrayal created such a sensation that other *bel canto* operas with mad scenes were quickly revived. Those by Vincenzo Bellini, *I Puritani* and *La Sonnambula,* musically lovely as their mad scenes are (though the one in *I Puritani* sounds uncannily like "Annie Laurie"), are not really in the running dramatically, since Bellini makes the cardinal mistake of restoring his heroines to sanity. As we all know, one of the great rules of mad scenes is that they should provide a convincing, thrilling means of killing off the operatic heroine. It will not do, for instance, to have Bellini's sleepwalker cross a perilous bridge while sound asleep and then merely *wake up,* when all the while we have been hoping that she will attempt dozens of dizzying roulades, hit the high E-flat, and then plunge off the bridge onto a mattress concealed below. Consequently, the palm for the second best female mad scene in opera must go to Giuseppe Verdi's earliest Shakespearean opera, *Macbeth.* Lady Macbeth's sleepwalking scene, while disappointingly short of a climactic nosedive, and lacking the E-flat finale, is nevertheless so psychologically compelling and moving in its quiet intensity (especially when performed by a real singing actress like Leonie Rysanek or Shirley Verrett) that this scene is almost as thrilling as the Lucia mad scene. Still, it *does* lack that lovely dialogue between soprano and flute—the original version of "Is it live, or is it Memorex?"

Frozen
Pizza

A crusty issue

THE main problem seems to be cryogenic. Like TV dinners, pizzas consist of a lot of different things (dairy products, meat, vegetables, bread dough) that don't like to thaw and cook at the same rate. In most cases it seems that when the topping is done, the crust remains mushy. Or if the crust is done, the cheese has turned to rubber and the vegetables to mush. Sometimes the pepperoni turns into tough little disks that would have to be pre-chewed by goats to be made palatable.

One popular solution adopted by many pizza manufacturers is to eliminate at least one of these problematic ingredients. Vegetables are usually the first to go, thus reducing the formula to crust, cheese and meat—"crust" being a somewhat vague term that might be anything ranging from the traditional unleavened dough to French bread and even (mama mia!) croissants.

Here, however, we feel compelled to draw the line. French bread may be, by logical extension, a sort of thick crust. But croissants with pizza stuffing are, we maintain, croissants with pizza stuffing and *not* pizzas. On the other hand, we can't ignore the traditional pizza calzone, which is a kind of pizza sandwich. In restaurants calzone is simply a pizza that has been folded in half before it's baked. Frozen-food manufacturers have managed to produce a version that looks like a big egg roll, but no matter; it's what's inside that counts.

Chicago Brothers Pizza is the best. Its thickness is not in the crust, but in the lush topping of cheeses, crisp vegetables, sauce, and meat. It's the closest thing to restaurant pizza we found in the frozen foods section, admirably spiced and beautiful to behold. But we did find it a trifle finicky in the oven. You have to watch it very carefully to achieve that fine balance of fully baked, crisp crust and perfectly (but not overly) cooked topping.

Purists might have grounds for challenging our choice for second best, but, as we said right up front, we do consider French bread to be a legitimate pizza crust. (Pizza, after all, is still in a state of evolution, having begun in Italy as a simple side dish and developed in the United States into a full-blown main course with no limit to its extravagant variations.) Stouffer's French Bread Pizza is crisp and light, loaded with five different kinds of cheese and—best of all—crisp vegetables which taste amazingly fresh (including yellow zucchini, zucchini, carrots, onions, and red pepper).

Honorable mention must be made of Michael Angelo's Calzone, even if it does look like an egg roll. The generous amounts of ricotta cheese and rich pepperoni sauce in this recipe produce a very pleasing result. What's more, it actually resembles the picture on the package.

Golf
Course

Perfect to a tee

ALL modern golf courses share a single ancestor: the Old Course of the Royal and Ancient Club of St. Andrews, in Fife, Scotland. In continuous use since 1754, its fairways were formed by the feet of golf's pioneers as they hacked their way through the gorse and heather, along sandy tracks, in search of ball and green. The irregular approaches, gently rolling hills, and devious hazards that make up every contemporary course descend from Scotland's "shrine of the game." Lord Lichfield, British society photographer and cousin of Queen Elizabeth II, calls the Old Course "*the* best."

The designers who built this country's first courses around the turn of the century were guided by the stingy Scots principle that a lousy shot should be heavily penalized. One of their earliest creations, the Pine Valley course at Clementon, New Jersey, is one gigantic sand trap broken by patches of fairway only slightly larger than the greens. Clumps of dense undergrowth provide ideal cover for fugitive Titleists, Spaldings, and Top Flights. "It is all very well to punish a bad stroke," wrote the esteemed golf writer, Bernard Darwin (Charles's grandson), after a hellish encounter with the approach to Pine Valley's eighth hole, "but the right of eternal punishment should be reserved for a higher tribunal than a Green Committee." Writer Charles Price called it "one big two-hundred-acre, unraked bunker." It is considered one of the best examples of penal design and the ultimate experience for target golfers, though it tends to have a demoralizing effect on the uninitiated.

As the sport grew in popularity, course designs grew more attractive, emphasizing the beauty of local landscapes. Fairways became vast fields of green that less skillful players could enjoy, while bestowing rewarding lies on better golfers. The master of this strategic design philosophy was Alister MacKenzie who, along with player Bobby Jones, designed the magnificently pastoral Augusta National. Laid out in the grounds of a 365-acre floral nursery in the early thirties, the fairways are emerald green, the sand traps white as snow, and the "rough" a blaze of azaleas that bloom every April just in time for the Masters' Tournament.

Then there are the heroic-design courses built by Robert Trent Jones (no relation to Bobby) that combine the grace and beauty of the strategic design with the challenge of the penal approach. Jones's courses feature many attractive but unforgiving water hazards that tempt expert players to drive across, if they dare, but allow more timid golfers to play around. The Point O' Woods Golf and Country Club at Benton Harbor, Michigan, is a beautiful example of Jones's work. Another is the Discovery Bay Golf Club in Hong Kong, considered the best course in Asia.

Cypress Point Golf Club, Pebble Beach, California, may be the finest example of the heroic design, though the layout was dictated more by nature than by the intentions of architects. The fairways curve around precipitous ocean cliffs, and water hazards include plumes of surf and tidal pools. This is a tough course, highly rated by the pros, but its wild and rough beauty make it a memorable experience for lesser mortals.

The Quinto Do Lago at Almansil, Algarve, Portugal, may be the finest club on the Continent. It is esteemed equally for its fairways of immaculately groomed Bermuda grass and the cuisine served in the clubhouse. Then there are the dew-kissed greens of the Emerald Isle, where there are more golf courses per capita than in any other country in the world. Two of the finest are the Tralee Golf Club, which features an intriguing hazard in the form of a crumbling castle ruin, and the Ballybunion Golf Club, where a frustrated Tom Watson, who just couldn't seem to get the course right, is said to have played furiously into the twilight hours.

Those are the courses that, worldwide, are the preferred dueling grounds of the pros and the knowledgeable amateurs who have the time and the money to play there. One day, our nomination for second best may rank with those courses. But because it's still relatively unknown, you don't need an invitation from a member, and you don't need to place your reservation for a tee-off time days or even weeks in advance. Praised by professional golfers *and* the Sierra Club (though it will be years before its landscape fully matures), Desert Highlands Golf Course near Phoenix, Arizona, was designed by none other than Jack Nicklaus.

This desert oasis of a golf course wraps around a stark mountain of red rock called Pinnacle Peak. Bands of desert sand crisscross fairways bordered by a collection of exotic cacti. An elaborate drainage system insulates the delicate desert environment from the irrigation system. Nicklaus believes each hole should present an inviting prospect to the golfer, luring him down a path that, if skillfully played, will be richly rewarded not only by a good lie but by a beautiful view of a landscape in which nature and the work of the architect are indistinguishable. "You're going to hear a lot about this course," Nicklaus says. Remember where you heard it first.

Graffito

*"Fortunatus made it
with Anthusam"*

Maybe it's something in the nature of walls themselves. "Something there is that doesn't love a wall," said Robert Frost, but he wasn't contemplating the interior surfaces of a toilet stall when he composed that thought. Perhaps walls are to us the most basic manifestation of social control and therefore prompt a primal sense of rebellion. But it's probably not so much the urge to deface as it is the need to be secret sharers of our wit and fancy. "All of us are sitting in the toilet but some of us are writing on the walls," wrote one insightful graffitist on the wall of a public lavatory in Scotland, in a variation on Oscar Wilde's famous line, "We are all in the gutter but some of us are looking at the stars."

Psychologists see graffiti as clues to the nature of our fantasies. To politicians they are a secret ballot box where the true feelings of a constituency may be safely uttered. To comedians they are a source of wit that reaches deep into an audience's libido. And among contemporary artists graffiti are now art—especially in the work of Keith Haring.

Sex is certainly a major theme. "Fortunatus made it with Anthusam," found on a wall in Pompeii and dating back certainly no later than A.D. 79, is a message of profound universality—but lacking in the kind of originality we admire. Better (and our nomination for best in the category of ancient graffito) is "copulate for coexistence," also found on a Pompeian wall and certainly remarkable both for its economy of expression and for its resemblance to a popular sixties slogan of similar sentiment.

In fact, the revolutionary sloganeering of the sixties produced many earnest graffiti, but the French managed to imbue their calls to the barricades with a poetic touch rarely found on West Coast campuses or on the walls of the East Village. Here are our favorites, found in Nanterre in the tumultuous month of May 1968: "I love you!!! Oh! Say it with paving stones!!!" and "Very soon there will be charming ruins."

Then there is that genre of graffito that is essentially a commentary on the nature of graffito itself. Our favorite is on a wall on University Avenue in Berkeley, California. There in bold crimson letters ten feet tall, some university wit has spray-painted the words:

JUST ANOTHER SENSELESS ACT OF VANDALISM

For second best we nominate not the wittiest or pithiest, but surely the most influential literary graffito. It contains no inherent grace elevating it above anything more than a bit of run-of-the-mill clever wordplay by some undergraduate English lit major. But to playwright Edward Albee, who encountered these words while in a Cambridge toilet stall, the effect was pure inspiration: "Who's afraid of Virginia Woolf?"

Greek Island

Honeymoon spot of the gods

In the Ionian Sea (between Greece and Italy) there's Corfu, Lawrence Durrell's *Prospero's Cell*. Unlike the Cyclades to the east, Corfu (or Kérkyra) is a green island, densely forested with olive trees punctuated by cypress spires and whitewashed, cubist mountain villages.

During the springtime festival of St. Spyridion, the mummified remains of the festival's namesake are carried through Corfu Town on a sedan chair, out of which two holy feet protrude, assuring the islanders of the saint's continued presence. Later, for reasons which are obscure, the townspeople throw all their crockery into the street.

The area south of the town is a sort of miniature Côte d'Azur of yacht harbors, casinos, and world-class hotels. But there are enough beaches left over for lesser budgets. Travel agents have a point when they nominate Corfu as the best.

Mykonos, at first glance, seems a perfect example of Cycladic simplicity. But the charming windmills and the stark blue and white of sea, sky, and architecture come to seem, on closer inspection, a parody of themselves—the sort of place Disney Studios would design for the island corner of "Greekworld." Better is Santorini (or Thíra), a volcanic half-moon cliff of an island rumored to be the site of antediluvian Atlantis and the source of the eruption that destroyed that civilization and caused all those problems for Noah. Unfortunately, the beaches are black and too hot to walk on, and if that's not bad enough, lately they've been overrun by photographers from New York shooting advertisements for Calvin Klein underwear.

Our choice for best of second best, therefore, is Samos, another green island just off the Turkish coast. The northernmost of the Sporades groups that includes the more frequently visited Rhodos and Paros, Samos is also known as Hera's Isle. Local legend maintains that Hera brought Zeus here for their honeymoon and, to prolong the bridal night, bribed the sun not to rise. After three centuries of connubial bliss, an exhausted Zeus (never a great intellect) grew suspicious of the prolonged darkness, discovered Hera's ruse, and forcefully demanded that the sun get back on the job. The experience put a strain on the marriage from which it never fully recovered.

Samos was also the home of the dictator Polycrates and the mathematician Pythagoras (who, besides creating the theorem about right-angled triangles, taught his followers that the souls of men reside in beans and adjured them never to pick up anything they dropped).

Between Samos's two mountains is the Valley of the Nightingales, a rich agricultural area famous for its olives, grapes, and bananas (yes, bananas), from which an excellent banana liqueur is made. A short cruise across the straits is the Turkish seaport of Kusadisi, dominated by a massive caravan fortress that encloses an oasis. Just north of there are the ruins of Ephesus, which many visitors find grander than the Acropolis.

Samos has a colorful yacht harbor, Pythagorean, overlooked by the squat remains of a crusader fortress. Similarly breathtaking are the many mountain villages, still relatively untouched by time, their only visible concessions to the modern age being the solar collectors on their red tiled roofs. Another striking feature of the local architecture is the overhanging balcony, a legacy of Turkish domination.

When Lord Byron exclaimed, "The isles of Greece! The isles of Greece!" he was probably thinking of Samos.

Guess as to Who Wrote Shakespeare's Plays

The Swan of Oxford

THE best guess is that Shakespeare's plays were written by William Shakespeare (1564–1616), suspected deer poacher, actor in a traveling show, and proud owner of New Place in his native Stratford-upon-Avon. And, indeed, by some it *is* regarded as a guess.

"Of all the immortal geniuses of literature, none is personally so elusive as William Shakespeare," writes Hugh Trevor-Roper (Lord Dacre of Glanton), the former Regius Professor of History at Oxford.

During his lifetime nobody claimed to know him. Not a single tribute was paid to him at his death. As far as the records go, he was uneducated, had no literary friends, possessed at his death no books, and could not write. It is true, six of his signatures have been found, all spelled differently: but they are so ill-formed that some graphologists suppose his hand to have been guided. Except for these signatures, no syllable of writing by Shakespeare has been identified. Seven years after his death, when his works were collected and published, and other poets claimed to have known him, a portrait of him was painted. The unskillful artist has presented the blank face of a country oaf.

Though we are sometimes told that Shakespeare's life is as well documented as could be expected, and even that it is one of the *best*-documented Elizabethan lives, we have only a few ambiguous scraps of information regarding him. The scholarly lives are often little less conjectural in their details than Anthony Burgess's novel *Nothing Like the Sun*. We have Christopher Marlowe's table talk and references to Edmund Spenser at Cambridge, but no positive evidence that Shakespeare ever spent a day inside a classroom, and not a single authenticated anecdote in which he is present in the role of an author. The Shakespeare who retired to Stratford, bought New Place, and left his second best bed to Anne Hathaway—the tax-evading, litigious Shakespeare whose doings are documented, albeit sparsely—often appears a coldhearted, grasping, money-mad provincial.

On the evidence of the poems and the plays, Shakespeare must have been "highly educated, even erudite" (Trevor-Roper), his head full of echoes from Ovid, Plautus, Virgil, Caesar, Sallust, and Cicero. He was evidently knowledgeable about falconry, courtly politics and other aristocratic sports, navigation, rhetoric, Italian novels, English histories, Montaigne, and Seneca. "The plays are Elizabethan conquests of territory," as one scholar has said. Milton, who was highly educated, referred to Shakespeare as "fancy's child"—but Shakespeare's immense vocabulary of 15,000 words was twice as large as his. English is full of Shakespearean coinages, usually derived from Latin roots.

Charlton Ogburn, a skeptic of Shakespeare's authorship, puts the matter succinctly: "How do orthodox scholars assimilate this vast reading to the life of the Stratfordian 'Shakspere' who arrived in London from the literary desert of a provincial town, presumably without means, speaking the crude Warwickshire dialect, harassed to support himself and three dependents at home, the craft of acting to learn, including dueling (before experts) and dancing, parts to memorize by the dozen . . . ?"

"Orthodox" scholars reply that only a fool or a snob would raise such a question—Shakespeare was simply a quick study. Yet there have been many famous doubters, including Walt Whitman, Mark Twain, Charles Chaplin, Benjamin Disraeli, Charles de Gaulle, Sigmund Freud, and Malcolm X. Henry James referred to the historical Shakespeare as "the lout from Stratford." But if the "lout" didn't write *Hamlet* and *Lear,* who did? And why did he cover up his identity?

Francis Bacon was the favorite choice of dissenters in the nineteenth century, when the question of Shakespeare's authorship was first raised. Claims have also been filed on behalf of Christopher Marlowe, the Earl of Derby, Sir Walter Raleigh, a committee including some or all of the above, Good Queen Bess, Michel Angelo Florio (father of John Florio, the translator of Montaigne), "Anne Whateley" (who was probably not a person at all but a scribal error), Anne Hathaway, and the Earl of Southampton.

Common sense aside, the problem for the Baconians is that we know too much about Lord Bacon. We have voluminous examples of his writings, and on stylistic grounds alone it is impossible to believe that the author of the *Essays* wrote the plays. The problem with Marlowe is that he was dead when the major plays were written. (See the entry for "Second Best Elizabethan Playwright.") Admittedly, this difficulty vanishes if one assumes, as his adherents do, that Marlowe's murder in a barroom brawl was faked by the spymaster Sir Francis Walsingham, his sometime employer and, according to the theory, his lover as well. Walsingham is supposed to have had Marlowe smuggled into France, just in time to avoid trial on charges of treason and sexual deviance. There the grateful poet dedicated the sonnets to him ("Mr. W. H." = Francis "Walsing-Ham").

The second best guess was first ventured by the unfortunately named J. Thomas Looney, an English schoolmaster from Gateshead. Looney's method was inductive. Persuaded that "Shakspere" couldn't possibly have written Shakespeare for all the reasons given above, he came up with a list of requirements that the real author, as he revealed himself in the works, would have to satisfy, such as being a genius, a recognized lyric poet, an aristocrat, "loose and improvident in money matters," fond of Italy, etc.—and then he set out to find the Elizabethan who fit the bill.

Edward de Vere, seventeenth Earl of Oxford, hereditary Lord Great Chamberlain of England, was born at Castle Hedingham, Essex, in 1550—one year before John Shakespeare, the supposed poet's father, was fined for keeping a dunghill in front of his house in Stratford-upon-Avon—and he died of the plague in 1604, six years before *The Tempest* is usually taken to have been composed and around the time "Willielmus Shexpere" was suing a Stratford druggist for a bad loan. Not only was Oxford an aristocrat, he was one of the most notable and learned of the courtier-poets. His entry in the *Dictionary of National Biography,* which Looney read with mounting excitement, says that he was grounded in Latin and French, an avid sportsman, possessed a "natural taste for music and literature," but was wayward and temperamental. He quarreled constantly with his all-powerful father-in-law, Lord Burghley. Queen Elizabeth adored him, but he enraged her as well. His plays were published, and two contemporary critics said he was "best for comedy" of anyone then writing. On occasion he displayed a "violent and perverse temper," like Hamlet; he had a marriage that tormented him, like Othello; and three daughters, like Lear. Of course, once the identification was made, all sorts of biographical parallels began to suggest themselves. For example, the detailed knowledge of Italian geography displayed in *The Merchant of Venice* and elsewhere is explained by de Vere's visit to that country in 1575–76. Polonius is his despised father-in-law, Burghley; Horatio, his cousin Horace, etc.

Moreover, the Earl was stagestruck. The *D. N. B.* notes that he was the patron of a company of players and "squandered some part of his fortune upon men of letters whose bohemian mode of life attracted him." According to the theory, his high place in the world, not to mention the personal and topical references hidden in the plays, made it impossible for him to be known as a working playwright, but his authorship was an open secret at court and among the literati. Hiring a bumpkin from Stratford to pose as "Shakespeare" was on the order of an inside joke.

Freud, a convinced Oxfordian, wrote that Shakespeare "seems to have nothing at all to justify his claim [i.e., to being the author of the plays], whereas Oxford has almost everything." The latest and most voluminous statement of the case for Oxford is Ogburn's *The Mysterious William Shakespeare: The Myth and the Reality* (1984), and very lively and well-written it is. In spite of all this, the world's English departments remain unconvinced, since, unfortunately, as the *D. N. B.* states, "although [Oxford] was a patron of a company of players, no specimen of his dramatic productions survives."

Now for an update. On September 25, 1987, a standing-room-only crowd at American University in Washington, D.C., watched as three sitting justices of the U.S. Supreme Court (William Brennan, Harry Blackmun, and John Paul Stevens) presided over a mock trial disputing "Shakspere's" versus de Vere's claim to be Shakespeare. "Shakspere" won—a foregone conclusion, though Justice Stevens admitted to a "gnawing uncertainty," and Justice Blackmun allowed that "even accepting [as] fact that 'Shakspere' was *not* the author," it was not proven that Oxford was. The press was decidedly less generous to the noble lord. The *New York Times* described him as "thoroughly dislikable," while the *Los Angeles Times* editorialized that the late plays could never have been written by someone who was not only "a notorious tosspot and a rakehell" but, at the time of their composition, dead to boot.

History of
the World in
One Volume

*"More about Tuscany
than Tobago"*

S IR Walter Raleigh (or Ralegh)
composed his *History of the World*
in a cell in the Tower of London.
Polymath, pirate, New World explorer, courtier—of all the Elizabethan courtier-poets "the most lofty,
insolent and passionate," according
to a contemporary account, Raleigh
was a dazzling character. Historian
Hugh Trevor-Roper describes him
as "the outrageous intellectual, the
arrogant courtier, rich, elegant, flam-
boyant, with his satin clothes and huge
pearl earrings." According to legend,
it was he who spread his cloak over a
puddle so that Elizabeth, the Virgin
Queen, wouldn't muddy her feet.
Reprieved from a death sentence for
treason, Raleigh spent twelve years

in the Tower, followed by a fateful voyage to the Orinoco, a second death sentence, and finally execution. Admiring his *sprezzatura,* we'd like to nominate Raleigh's incomplete *History* as best, or second best, but unfortunately, it was first published in 1614, and a lot has happened since then. (But then, a good case could be made that history should have ended in 1614.)

Arguably the greatest history written in the twentieth century is Fernand Braudel's two-volume *The Mediterranean and the Mediterranean World in the Age of Philip II* (1959; revised edition, 1973), a magnificent work comparable in sweep and erudition to Gibbon or Macaulay. Braudel is the master of the French "Annaliste" school of historians (so called for their journal, *Annales*). The Annalistes tend to despise mere dates, battles, and lists of kings—narrative history of the kind practiced by historians from Thucydides to Barbara Tuchman—as heartily as any schoolboy. Their dream is to detect the inner structures behind events, slow, glacial changes and the interplay of geography with humankind, in a true "global" history.

However, of the kind of one-volume history of humankind that takes you from the pharaohs to Ronald Reagan in a few hundred readable pages, the more prosaic and fact-minded Brits have almost a monopoly. *Almost,* we say, because standing head and shoulders over all the other entrants in this category is *The Rise of the West,* by William H. McNeill of the University of Chicago, quite simply the best history of the world in one volume. It was first published in 1964 and was named the winner of the National Book Award for that year.

Arnold Toynbee described McNeill's 896 pages as "the most lucid presentation of world history in narrative form that I know"—high praise coming from a historian who seems to have read everything in print since Gutenberg. Trevor-Roper (a savage critic of Toynbee) chimed in with some lavish praise of his own, pronouncing *The Rise of the West* "not only the most learned and the most intelligent, also the most stimulating and fascinating book that has ever set out to recount and explain the whole history of mankind." Despite the book's title, McNeill takes all history as his province, including the arts and technology, and he makes high drama of the slow welding of East and West into a single global civilization.

Among the Britons competing for second best, Toynbee himself and J. M. Roberts deserve honorable mention. Toynbee became world-famous for his immense *Study of History* (the title is the only modest thing about it), that came out in twelve volumes between 1934 and 1961. His vogue had passed by the time he wrote his one-volume *Mankind and Mother Earth,* which has been underrated for that reason. Nonetheless, it's lucid, grand in scope, and a good read.

Roberts's *Penguin History of the World* is immensely learned and ambitious, solid, reliable, and pedestrian of prose. An Oxford don, Roberts has written with panache on such arcane subjects as the mythology of the Illuminati and other secret societies, but his world history has a summary, textbookish quality we find off-putting. It is only fair to say that his fellow professionals think very highly indeed of Roberts's volume. A. J. P. Taylor pronounced it "a stupendous achievement . . . the unrivaled World History for our day." The late J. H. Plumb called it "the most outstanding history of the world yet written."

Still, we prefer Hugh Thomas's *History of the World,* originally published in England with the more appropriate and modest title, *An Unfinished History of the World.* Lord Thomas is chairman of the Center for Policy Studies, a conservative, free-market think tank in England with strong ties to the Thatcher government. His other books, such as *The Suez Affair, The Spanish Civil War,* and *Armed Truce* (about the origins of the Cold War), are essays in recent history; and to retelling the story of mankind he brings journalistic flair and urgency. He doesn't think Europe is finished, and he is unabashed about stressing the importance of England's role in the last four hundred years. (Which is okay with us. Within living memory, the British flag flew over one-quarter of the earth's surface.)

"It will become evident that the 'world' mentioned in the title is not so large as some would expect," Thomas confesses. "There is more here about Tuscany than Tobago." But he compensates for his "Eurocentrism" with expert treatment of technology, and a concern, formerly rare in this kind of book, with the lives of ordinary people—what used to be known as "the short and simple annals of the poor." A chapter on the Industrial Revolution, for example, is titled simply "How Long Did They Work?" (Answer: for a typical English factory worker in 1849 it was 73.5 hours a week. Only stock-market analysts still work that hard—or, at any rate, that long.)

As the second best history of the world in one volume, Thomas's *Unfinished History* is quirky, provocative, flawed (the proofreader should have been shot), but equal to its grand theme.

Hollywood Film Director

The Kenosha Kid

Iᴛ is not true that David Wark Griffith invented the close-up, the traveling shot, and crosscutting, as is sometimes said. It *is* true that Griffith was an appalling sentimentalist and an old-fashioned racist (in *The Birth of a Nation*, the Ku Klux Klansmen are the heroes); and it is also true that the director of *The Birth of a Nation*, *Intolerance*, and *Broken Blossoms* is esteemed by most critics as the greatest director ever to work in Hollywood or anywhere else. As Andrew Sarris says in his classic survey *The American Cinema: Directors and Directions, 1929–1968*, "The cinema of Griffith is no more outmoded, after all, than the drama of

Aeschylus. The debt that all filmmakers owe to D. W. Griffith defies calculation." But second best?

In his book, Sarris examines the oeuvres of over two hundred directors, ranging from Jean Renoir to Jerry Lewis, Rex Ingram to Marlon Brando (he directed *One-Eyed Jacks* in 1961), slotting them into such categories as "The Far Side of Paradise," "Expressive Esoterica," and "Strained Seriousness." At the top of the heap he lists the "Pantheon Directors," "who have transcended their technical problems with a personal vision of the world. To speak any of their names is to evoke a self-contained world with its own laws and landscapes." They are:

Charles Chaplin	Fritz Lang
Robert Flaherty	Ernst Lubitsch
John Ford	F. W. Murnau
D. W. Griffith	Max Orphuls
Howard Hawks	Jean Renoir
Alfred Hitchcock	Josef von Sternberg
Buster Keaton	Orson Welles

This is a mixed bag, to say the least. (But we don't think any of the younger directors are—as yet—ready for Pantheon status.)

Flaherty, the lone documentarist, invites you to step inside igloos and grass shacks (*Nanook of the North, Tabu*); von Sternberg is more at home in palaces (*The Scarlet Empress*) and depraved Weimar Republic nightclubs (*The Blue Angel*). Fritz Lang (*Metropolis, M, Fury*) was a moody Teutonic expressionist, dramatizing paranoia and panic. His contemporary Ernst Lubitsch (*Ninotchka, Heaven Can Wait*) was master of the discreet sex farce. John Ford's career lasted fifty years; Murnau, who virtually invented modern camera movement, was dead at forty.

Chaplin's phenomenal popularity has never been equaled—not by the Beatles, not by Elvis. Howard Hawks (*Bringing Up Baby, Red River*) was for most of his career ignored even by cineasts. Welles was world famous before he was thirty, but in consequence bore the label of "aging *enfant terrible*" like a leper's bell for the rest of his days.

And it's with the late enfant terrible (b. Kenosha, 1915; d. Los Angeles, 1986) that we'll go for second best. *Citizen Kane* is ritually voted the "Greatest Film of All Time" in surveys of film critics. As Sarris says, "*Citizen Kane* is still the work that influenced the cinema more profoundly than any American film since *Birth of a Nation.*" Welles revolutionized the movie sound track with the tricks he'd learned as director of radio's "Mercury Theater," and he changed the look of the movies by reviving the brooding, expressionistic camera work of the twenties. According to François Truffaut, "Everything that matters in cinema since 1940 has been influenced by *Citizen Kane* and Jean Renoir's *La Règle de Jeu.*"

It's interesting that apart from the comedians Chaplin and Keaton, Welles, himself an actor of genius, is the only one on the list who achieved glory for anything except film direction. As a twenty-three-year-old theatrical prodigy, famed for such productions as his "voodoo" *Macbeth,* he was on the cover of *Time* magazine (May 1938) before he ever directed a movie. Everyone knows how his radio adaptation of H. G. Wells's *The War of the Worlds* panicked millions of listeners into believing the Martians had landed.

By the time he was thirty, as his biographer Charles Higham observes, Welles was a revolutionary artist working in three different media— radio, theater, and movies. His career as an actor spanned fifty years. On stage, he played Othello, Captain Ahab, and Dr. Faustus in his own productions. In an irony he did not relish, his most famous performance on film was not in one of his own pictures but as the glamorous crook, Harry Lime, in Carol Reed's (a strum of the zither here) *The Third Man.*

Welles's two great Hollywood movies are *Citizen Kane* and *The Magnificent Ambersons,* the latter a "mutilated masterpiece," as François Truffaut called it, cut by RKO after a disastrous preview and released with a tacked-on happy ending. To these, many critics would add the baroque thriller *The Lady from Shanghai,* starring Rita Hayworth (Welles's second wife). Though he had powerful admirers, the young Welles was never popular in Hollywood—he was never forgiven for the unprecedented freedom his first studio contract gave him, and *Citizen Kane* was booed when it was voted best screenplay at the Academy Awards in 1940. And the commercial failure of *The Magnificent Ambersons,* among other sins, made him damaged goods in the eyes of the moguls. During his long European exile, he completed, among many aborted or unfinished projects, *Othello* and *Chimes at Midnight,* in which he played Falstaff, his favorite role.

Welles's critics and biographers continue to debate whether he was undone by Hollywood or by his own deep streak of self-destructiveness. There is even an academic cottage industry devoted to the question of whether he stole the credit for the screenplay of *Citizen Kane* from Herman Mankiewicz.

Welles's great themes were childhood tragedy (as the critic André Bazin discerned), death, and the moral failings of the capitalist society which obdurately made him rich and famous. As Higham notes, "Ironically, while the films he directed were failing, Welles himself was highly bankable as an actor and public personality. . . ."

At the time of his death—by then best known as the Zeppelin-sized huckster for Paul Masson ("No wine before its time!") and as a talk-show raconteur and living legend with a permanently reserved table at Ma Maison—Welles was obstinately preparing a film of *King Lear* and another based on *The Cradle Will Rock,* one of his early theater triumphs. Inside the Grand Old Man, the marvelous boy who directed *Citizen Kane* at twenty-five was still screaming to be let out. "I can't help making things into movies," he told his authorized biographer Barbara Leaming. "They just don't let me make them!"

Home Video Entertainment Center

It's no longer just a TV

TELEVISION sets are the ubiquitous measure of membership in the electronic age. There are more TVs per household in this country than there are toilets or refrigerators. The average American television set is turned on six to eight hours a day. And, of course, some critics argue that what we experience in front of our flickering screens is a state of being that resembles nothing so much as a coma.

Perhaps that is why television sets never rose to the same state-of-the-art level as stereo systems or home computers. But all that is changing now. Manufacturers are loading the latest models with high-tech features, stereo sound is finally available (just in time for the baroque decline of MTV), and viewers are using their sets in ways not even Ernie Kovacs could have anticipated.

TV sets are becoming the central components of systems that include such "peripherals" as VCRs, videodisc players, home computers, DBS receivers, cable decoders, and potentially interactive videotext channels. Which, of course, makes manufacturers very happy because instead of selling you just the set, they now have a line of gadgets that stretches from here to the limit on your MasterCard.

The introduction of digital technology helps keep the prices of your home video entertainment center down (microchips are cheaper and more reliable than tubes), and it makes a whole range of appealing improvements possible. The most advanced feature (not yet widely available) is the ability to display on the screen an inset that contains a separate signal. Unfortunately, very few sets can actually receive more than one signal at a time, but if yours does have this feature, you can use it with your VCR or videodisc components (future receivers will eventually have multiple-tuning capability). Picture clarity is greatly enhanced on digital sets because of their ability to "store" individual frames and hold them for a few microseconds until the next frame is complete. Also, those annoying ghost images are eliminated because sets can sense when signals are weak or overlapping and automatically seek out the strongest signal and boost it, while ignoring the "echoes." Further refinements are stop-frame and zoom capabilities, which will add a new dimension to viewing, particularly when it comes to second-guessing referees. And, of course, you can control the whole system with your digital remote control.

The heart of the home video system is, of course, a large-screen color television. There are currently over two hundred models of large-screen (25"–27") TVs on the market, supplied by twenty-seven manufacturers; most of these have some or all of the latest digital features. Sony, Magnavox, Panasonic, Philco, JVC, Quasar, Mitsubishi, Zenith, RCA, and General Electric have consistently turned out the highest-quality sets, and the investments they've made in research have kept their products on the cutting edge of video technology. But while our choice for second best doesn't have a name commonly associated with high-tech electronics, one reliable independent survey rates it right alongside the top ten.

Consumer Reports listed almost two hundred models and rated the top eighteen. Among the best was, believe it or not, Montgomery Ward's 17737. Their only criticism of the model was that its signal reception was easily disrupted by low-flying aircraft. But for the features it offers (at a price below most of the equivalent competition), we're willing to endure a little airplane flutter. The Ward's remote control may lack the fine-tuning capability of its brand-name competitors, but that's not as important to us as picture quality, and in that category it equals or excels the rest. Other features include stereo/SAP decoder with stereo speakers, quartz tuner, automatic fine tuner, sixty-six-channel reception (VHS and UHF), sharpness control, coaxial jack for cable and VHF antennae, room-light sensor, infrared remote control, and tone and stereo balance controls.

Horror
Movie

Don't look now!

FRIGHT-FLICK devotee Carlos Clarens, author of *An Illustrated History of the Horror Film,* put it best: "The Western is a lost art and the musical is a lost cause, but horror movies live forever; they keep coming back, after death at the box office, on cable and cassettes."

This genre is rooted in Grand Guignol and Gothic romances, and shades over on either side to supernaturalism (e.g., *The Exorcist*) and science fiction (e.g., *Alien*). (*Alien* made us wish Carl Sagan would ask for an RSVP in all those invitations he keeps posting into outer space.)

One of the best descriptions of what horror movies are all about was ventured by Freud in his essay, "Das

Unheimlich," in which he notes that the "uncanny" can be defined as "something which ought to have remained hidden but has come to light." Not only are horror films more horrific than ever before, what with the sunshine boys Jason (*Friday the 13th* and its many sequels), Michael (*Halloween*), and Freddy (*Nightmare on Elm Street*) dreaming up ever grislier ways to axe to death, bludgeon, impale, and eviscerate oversexed, underbrained teenagers, but now we must also contend with the creepy, eczematous vision of cult favorites David Lynch (*Eraserhead*) and David Cronenberg (*The Brood, The Fly*). *Newsweek* critic Jack Kroll says that Lynch's theme in *Eraserhead* is nothing less than "the ultimate corruption of matter itself throughout the universe." That's something to think about in the front row.

Few genres have ever produced so much well-loved dreck as the horror movie in its Eisenhower age of innocence. The riotous *Plan 9 from Outer Space* was elected "The Worst Film of All Time" in Michael and Harry Medved's poll for the *Golden Turkey Awards,* though a close runner-up in our view (it also placed with the Medveds' readers) is the somewhat later *Horror of Party Beach,* in which radioactive sea slime decides to do something about a surplus population of hunks and bunnies on the California oceanfront. Equally memorable is *The Blob,* which pitched Steve McQueen into battle with an oozy puddle of bloodred goo. (Remember the scene when the blob started pouring into a movie theater from the air-conditioning vents?) *From Hell It Came,* another clunker, features a Margaret Mead-like anthropologist, the walking dead, and a marauding tree named Tabonga. In *Mesa of Lost Women,* Jackie Coogan stars as a demented scientist trying to breed spider women on an isolated Mexican plateau. This film is so stupefyingly bad, it has been mistaken for an acid flashback. Similar in plot is the tongue-in-cheek thriller praised by entomologists, *Invasion of the Bee Girls,* directed by Academy Award winner Denis Sanders. Needless to say, it was not for this picture that Sanders got his Oscars.

Two classy horror movies, Stanley Kubrick's *The Shining* and Jack

Clayton's *The Innocents* (with a screenplay by Truman Capote), were adapted, respectively, from a trashy novel by Stephen King (the adaptation by Diane Johnson was not to the demotic novelist's liking) and from Henry James's *The Turn of the Screw*. (Capote followed Edmund Wilson's interpretation, i.e., the ghosts aren't "real" but projected by the sexually repressed governess.) There are frissons in both. "H-e-e-e-re's John-n-n-ny!"

More generic gore in our top ten includes *Horror Express,* in which passengers on the Trans-Siberian Railway lose their souls to an H. P. Lovecraftian fiend stowed in the baggage compartment; *The Conqueror Worm,* a sixties cult classic directed by Michael Reeves, in which Vincent Price turns in a fine performance as a demented witch-hunter during the English civil war; the original *Invasion of the Body Snatchers,* best of the Eisenhower-era films about depersonalization; and the original *Night of the Living Dead.*

We're declaring the original sound versions of *Frankenstein, Dracula, King Kong,* and *The Mummy* hors de combat. Familiarity does not breed fright. (*Nosferatu,* F. W. Murnau's silent version of *Dracula,* remains a spine-tingler, however.) *Psycho* still tops our list of the films we wish our parents hadn't let us see, and we agree with Dennis Peary, who is to the cult film what T. S. Eliot was to metaphysical poetry, that John Carpenter's *Halloween* is "not only the scariest horror film since *Psycho,* but also the most imaginatively directed."

Our choice for second best predates *Psycho,* and if it isn't as shuddery as *Halloween* or *Horror Express,* or as broody and doomy as *Conqueror Worm,* or as repellent as *The Brood*—well, you really must see *I Married a Monster from Outer Space* (1958) for yourself. Long derided and still underestimated by critics, *IMAMFOS* depicts the marital problems of young Marge Farrell (Gloria Talbott) and her Bill (Tom Tryon), a kind-hearted regular guy who metamorphoses into a puppy-kicking teetotaling crank after they tie the knot. The explanation for his change is, of course, that Bill is really a hideous space alien.

I Married a Monster from Outer Space was directed and produced by Gene Fowler, Jr., a sometime film editor for Fritz Lang, and Peary detects a number of classy Langian tricks in the film, including "invisible" editing and expressionist camera angles. Apart from the mastery of suspense and atmospherics, the film is notable for the streak of black humor revealed in such scenes as the get-togethers of Bill and his alien friends in a local bar (allergic to alcohol, they order soft drinks and grouse about their dumb assignment to mate with Earth women in order to repopulate their plague-stricken planet Andromeda). Peary describes the film as "basically an intelligent, atmospheric, subtly made sci-fi thriller" unfortunately tagged with a ludicrous title. More than that, we think, it is a prophetic synthesis of the dominant themes of fifties horror films (nativist paranoia and fear of possession) with the brooding antisensuality that prevails today. At the film's end, when the aliens are ripped open by German shepherds, we see there are worse things than the skull beneath the skin—an anticipation of the gnostic terrors of Lynch and Cronenberg. And hey, *we* think the title is great. What did critics of the fifties think it should have been called—*Scenes from a Marriage*?

Hot Dog

Hot, hot, hot dog

THIS country long ago sacrificed quality for quantity in the manufacture of America's most populist sausage, but there are still a few makers of wieners who pride themselves in following the time-honored (and time-consuming) traditions needed to produce a superior frank.

Usingers of Milwaukee will sell no wiener before its time (at least three hours in the smoker, compared with ten to fifteen minutes for most commercial brands). And Chicago's Leonard Slotkowski makes a slow-smoked, natural-cased dog that is comparable in quality to its Milwaukee rival. Both are available in limited supply throughout the Midwest and South.

Then there is the William Paley hot dog. The man who created CBS and guided the broadcasting industry into the television era took time out from his on-again, off-again retirement to build a vest-pocket park in Manhattan, where he offers an all-beef wiener that is steamed and grilled and served on a bun brushed with melted butter. In an interview with *Quality* magazine, Paley says he spent a month sampling potential Paley dogs, "to make sure the hot dog we served would be the best ever made. As far as I'm concerned, the finest caviar in the world cannot compare with the American hot dog."

Nathan's, of course, makes a top-notch sausage that is available in its restaurants around New York City. And if only for sentimental reasons, it deserves its reputation as the hot dog by which all others are judged in this country.

But our nomination for second best is produced only in Berkeley and Oakland, alas, and (like Nathan's) is only available in a few restaurants. That is because Top Dogs, like Usingers, are made in limited quantity to control quality. The tiny Top Dog restaurants, plastered with libertarian propaganda, are shrines dedicated to The Experience of the Pure Sausage, and they are always crowded with the faithful. We particularly recommend their fiery Polish dog, in which one can savor a delicate blend of spices in that fraction of an instant before the pepper begins to detonate.

Ice Cream Bar

Bye-bye Eskimo Pie

THE BMW of ice cream bars is undoubtedly Häagen-Dazs. We don't care for the phony Scandinavian-sounding name, but the thick chocolate coating is the genuine article (from Belgium, home of Godiva chocolates), and the ice cream is rich and smooth.

Second best, and the probable inspiration for the Häagen-Dazs bar, is the tempting but frustrating DoveBar. The bittersweet outer chocolate of DoveBars is well matched with their creamy interior. Unfortunately this thick coating almost never breaks where you bite. The result is large chunks of DoveBar on your lap. Another problem is size. They're too big. Aside from the postprandial guilt, the immediate aftereffect is not unlike what wee Willie Wonka must have felt after a week or so in the chocolate factory. Too much of a good thing and impossible to share (but who would want to, anyway?). DoveBars are a tantalizing invitation to dining disaster.

Perhaps the reason Beverly Sills refuses to share desserts—one of the great lady's few idiosyncrasies—is because the desserts she prefers are the frustratingly, deliciously unshareable DoveBars.

Ice Cream Maker

The little chill

Is your idea of an ice cream maker something you prime with rock salt and crank—preferably, on Grandma's front porch, with a glass of homemade lemonade in your hand? Well, Grandma wouldn't even recognize the Italian-made Simac—the best—as an ice cream maker. This sleek, chic piece of Milanese design makes delectable, creamy ice cream in about twenty minutes. It also costs $450 and is the size of a small filing cabinet—not the kind of thing you bring to the table so your guests can watch.

Second best, lots cheaper, and more fun for kids is the Donvier. You actually have to crank the Donvier (which the kids like—didn't you?), but only a couple of times every two or three minutes, for fifteen to twenty minutes. You also have to remember to put the Donvier in the freezer for seven hours before use, to ice the Chillfast sealed inside. The one-quart model is about the size of a popcorn popper and costs a mere $40. It's made in Japan.

The *Iliad* and the *Odyssey* (Translation)

"But you must not call it Homer"

THE most famous translation of Homer into English is Alexander Pope's *Iliad* in rhymed couplets, which made Pope rich and was much admired by some of the best authorities. Dr. Johnson called it "a performance which no age or nation can pretend to equal." But such acclaim did not save the poet from suffering a definitive put-down when he demanded an opinion from Richard Bentley, the famous classical scholar: "A pretty poem, Mr. Pope, but you must not call it Homer."

George Chapman's version, which appeared between 1598 and 1616, inspired the Greekless John Keats's "On First Looking into Chapman's Homer," surely the handsomest tribute ever accorded a translation.

Then felt I like some watcher of the skies
 When a new planet swims into his ken;
Or like stout Cortez, when with eagle eyes
 He stared at the Pacific—and all his men
Looked at each other with a wild surmise—
 Silent, upon a peak in Darien.

(Yes, he should have written "stout *Balboa,*" but it wouldn't scan.)

 Nineteenth-century scholars were doubtful that the blind bard ever really existed and regarded both poems as a patchwork of epics by different creators. Contemporary classicists, however, are inclined to believe in a historical Homer who sang of Achilles' wrath in the courts of Asia Minor. The *Odyssey,* too, they regard as the work of a single poet, though perhaps not the same one. In the nineteenth century, the novelist Samuel Butler, and in the twentieth, the poet Robert Graves, believed that the author of the *Odyssey* was a woman. (Graves nominated the princess Nausikaa.)

 In this century, Homeric studies were revolutionized by Milman Perry's researches into "heroic recitation" in the Balkans. Now Homer is thought to have composed aloud, relying on traditional verbal formulas, a theory which makes him a different figure altogether from Pope's poet or from the subtle allegorist read by students at the Library of Alexandria two thousand years ago. As critic Hugh Kenner remarks, "Even our own Formulaic Homer is manifestly our own, a modern being unknown to Bentley or Jowett, let alone Aristotle, extrapolated by 20th-century minds from 20th-century researches in Yugoslavia."

 There are a lot of bad translations available. The popular Butcher and Lang translations of the nineteenth century belonged to the "O suitably attired in leather boots" school derided by A. E. Housman. Robert Fagles, himself a translator of the *Oresteia,* describes the best-selling translations of the *Odyssey* by W. H. D. Rouse (Mentor) and E. V. Rieu

(Penguin) as "the supposed rough-and-tumble campfire yarn of the first, the unctuous chitchat of the second."

The second best modern English translation of the *Iliad* is by Robert Fitzgerald, who did the best translation of the *Odyssey* (both published by Anchor Doubleday). The second best version of the *Odyssey* is by Richmond Lattimore, and he, by a nice symmetry, published the best version of the *Iliad* (both of his books are published by Harper and Row). Fitzgerald, a poet, became Boylston Professor of Rhetoric at Harvard. Lattimore, a longtime professor of classics at Bryn Mawr, was coeditor, with David Grene, of the magnificent *Chicago Complete Greek Tragedies*.

Lattimore's translation of the *Iliad* was the first to appear (1951), and among the critics singing its praises was Fitzgerald, who said: "The feat is so decisive that it is reasonable to foresee a century or so in which nobody will try again to put the *Iliad* in English verse." In time, however, the translator got the better of the critic. His own version of the *Odyssey* (1961) appeared to a chorus of praise quite as deafening as that which greeted Lattimore's *Iliad*. ("At last we have an *Odyssey* worthy of the original": William Arrowsmith.) Lattimore than leapfrogged him with a new *Odyssey* in 1965.

The *Iliad* and the *Odyssey* are very different poems. As George Steiner says, "The poet of the *Iliad* looks on life with those blank, unswerving eyes which stare out of the helmet slits on early Greek vases. His vision is terrifying in its sobriety, cold as the winter sun." Lattimore's version, which he then quotes, is calculated to capture precisely this antique Attic sobriety:

> *So, friend, you die also? Why all this clamour about it?*
> *Patroklos also is dead, who was better by far than you are.*

Without going in for the pseudo-archaisms that make nineteenth-century translations unreadable, Lattimore tries to approximate in modern English the alien rhythms and poetic formulas of Homer's Greek. Even the transliterations he prefers, like *Achilleus* and *Patroklos,* as opposed to the more familiar Latinized versions, have a spiky, Greekish look.

The *Odyssey* is by comparison ironical, novelistic, even alexandrine, more suited to Fitzgerald's subtler, sinuous, and sensual effects, or so (as Fagles implies in an important essay) Fitzgerald persuades us. (Lawrence of Arabia, who translated the *Odyssey* as "T. E. Shaw," called it the first European novel.) In the famous silent interview between Ulysses and Penelope in Book XXIII, Fitzgerald is quietly naturalistic:

And she, for a long time, sat deathly still
in wonderment—for sometimes as she gazed
she found him—yes, clearly—like her husband,
but sometimes blood and rags were all she saw.

Lattimore is grander but flatter:

She sat a long time in silence, and her heart was wondering.
Sometimes she would look at him, with her eyes full upon him,
and again would fail to know him in the foul clothing he wore.

The classicist H. A. Mason, who suggests this test case, reminds us what sort of thing earlier translators were capable of, and quotes Lawrence, who pictures Odysseus "waiting with dropping eyelids to hear his stately consort cry out." Mason notes the kittenish quality in Fitzgerald's translation, observing that it's the first version to make plausible Butler's idea that if a warrior might have written the *Iliad,* a woman must have written the *Odyssey*—we take that to be a compliment to Fitzgerald's virtuosity.

Since both Lattimore and Fitzgerald's translations are available in inexpensive paperback, the best thing is to buy both sets and set aside a summer to read them, preferably on a vacation in the Greek islands.

Italian
Ice Cream
Parlor

La dolce gelato

SOME say the Egyptians invented it; others claim that the recipe came from China, brought back (along with spaghetti) by Marco Polo. Whatever its origins, by the fourteenth century *gelato* (Italian for "ice cream") was firmly established on the Renaissance menus of Italy's city-states. Its preparation was, however, a jealously guarded secret, carefully preserved by the well-connected clans of the ruling class.

This monopoly lasted for nearly two hundred years until Catherine de' Medici smuggled the recipe to France in the sixteenth century and introduced it to the royal court. From there it spread throughout Europe and, in a somewhat corrupted form, reached the United States in the nineteenth century. Alas, however, the farther the recipe traveled, the less it resembled the marvelous delicacy—as Italian as pizza pie—that continued to be cherished in its homeland. But now comes the scoop: it took the political turmoil of the sixties and a connection between the American underground and Italy's Red Brigades to bring the real stuff to our shores.

We can't divulge the entire story, but this much we can say: an American activist, a member of a nationally known, ultraleft political action group, visited Italy in the late sixties to connect with radical groups there. When he wasn't plotting the downfall of the military-industrial complex, he visited gelaterias. Later his activism waned, but his fondness for gelato remained firm, and he channeled his subversive impulse into flooding the U.S. with this seductive foreign product. Measured in calories, his success is incalculable. The nationally franchised chain he founded is worth millions today, and rumor has it that he is a heavy supporter of the Democratic party.

There are gelaterias in every major American city, but only a handful produce the true gelato, free of preservatives and made fresh daily. There are four kinds: the easiest to find are *cremolati,* made with fresh egg yolks, cream, milk, sugar, and natural flavorings; and *sorbetto,* popularly called "Italian ice," concocted with fresh or fresh-frozen fruit. Less frequently encountered in this country are the subtly flavored *crema bianca,* prepared without the intrusive flavor of egg yolks, and the incredibly delicate *semi-freddo,* a hand-whipped combination of thick cream and cooked meringue.

The best gelaterias undoubtedly include the Bar Italia in St. Louis, which features unique fresh-fruit sorbettos in such flavors as papaya, kiwi, and mango; Big Alice's in Providence, which offers cremolati-style ice cream and sorbettos in such unique flavors as Russian Tea and prune; and—the only gelateria on our list that serves semi-freddo—Il Dolce Momento of Boston, San Diego, and Florence. The Florentine branch of Il Dolce Momento has twice won the prestigious "Best European Ice

Cream Award" in recent years; its American cooks study their art in Italy and make all their flavors by hand daily. One reviewer recently declared she felt she was eating whipped cream, so light and fluffy is Il Dolce Momento's semi-freddo.

For second best we have two nominations. Toscanini's of Cambridge, Massachusetts, whose grand, flavorful experiments reflect the intellectual curiosity of that academic community, has produced such treats as Avocado Ice, Cocoa Pudding Cremolati, and Gingersnap Molasses Cream. It limits the number of its offerings (only eight flavors daily) to allow time for experimentation. San Francisco's Vivoli, our other nomination, energetically produces a wide enough range of flavors to appease that city's eclectic tastes, from apricot to Zabiglione. Between them everyone should be able to find his or her idea of la dolce cremolati.

Import-Export Deal

OPEC imports oil

For almost a century the DeBeers company has controlled the world diamond market, hoarding vast quantities of African gems, and releasing a steady but niggardly trickle to keep prices high. DeBeers further enhanced the value of its holdings by creating the concept of the diamond engagement ring, spending millions each year to promote the idea. To keep prices stable, it arranged to sell to only one syndicate that would distribute the heavily promoted, artificially high-priced stones to the world's jewelers. So when in 1960 the Russians discovered an enormous diamond deposit in Siberia, DeBeers was worried.

The man in charge of DeBeers, Harry Oppenheimer, went to the Russians with a deal. As long as they sold only to him, he told them, the world supply could be kept under control and prices would remain high, guaranteeing the U.S.S.R. a steady income of much-needed foreign capital.

The only problem was DeBeers' status as a Rhodesian company. The Soviet Socialist Republic and the white minority-controlled capitalist government of Rhodesia weren't on speaking terms at the time. It wouldn't do for the strongest supporter of Rhodesia's rebel movement to be seen entering into an agreement that would enrich that country's wealthiest private company. So DeBeers agreed to keep the arrangement secret.

The deal has worked out well for both parties. When, after Rhodesia had metamorphosed into Zimbabwe, DeBeers was kicked out of its native country, Russia arranged for the new government to sell only to a DeBeers front company. The U.S.S.R. continues to get top dollar for its Siberian gems.

There's no doubt DeBeers and Russia make strange bedfellows, but for second best we salute Permaflex Ltd. of Stoke on Trent, England, for being the only company in the world that has succeeded in exporting large quantities of petroleum each year to the Arab states.

Permaflex manufactures lighter fluid, among other petroleum products, and in that form Saudi Arabia, Abu Dhabi, and other Middle East OPEC members buy back over $100,000 of oil annually. Rule Britannia!

Journal of Opinion

An American political tradition

The best American journal of opinion is *The New Republic* on a good week. We'd like to say second best is *The New Republic* on a bad week, but our editor will not hear of such nice discriminations. Second best, then, is the *Nation*, 120 years old, still left-wing as politics are defined in our United States, still printed on sincere, smudgy newsprint, and still capable of outraging "respectable" opinion.

First, let us praise *The New Republic* in its current incarnation, with Martin Peretz as editor in chief. When *TNR* celebrated its seventieth anniversary in 1984 with a fete at the National Portrait Gallery in Washington, D.C., the guests included

Katharine Graham, Jerry Brown, Eugene McCarthy, Henry Kissinger, Gary Hart, Fran Liebowitz, Senator Patrick Moynihan, Betty Friedan, and Jeane Kirkpatrick (a former contributor, who now writes for *Commentary*). But then, since 1914, when Herbert Croly was editor and the young Walter Lippmann was on the staff, *TNR* has been the house organ of American liberalism. Ex-liberal Ronald Reagan still subscribes.

Arthur M. Schlesinger, Jr.'s, description of the young *TNR* as "the voice of Eastern, metropolitan progressivism . . . intellectual, stylish, urbane," is not too far off the mark today—though the journal has gone through considerable changes since it began as the voice of Theodore Roosevelt's "New Nationalism." These include its embrace of Wilsonian internationalism and the New Deal, a flirtation with the Soviet Union (especially in the back pages), and a period of fuzzy thinking under the editorship of Henry Wallace.

Peretz, who bought the magazine for $380,000 in 1974, is widely perceived by the Left as steering it to the Right. Onetime contributor Noam Chomsky describes it as "a disgraceful and vulgar sheet," referring to what he sees as Peretz's intransigently pro-Israel stand. Such regulars as Charles Krauthammer have a weakness for Ronald Reagan. On the other hand, editor Michael Kinsley, who has taken over the "T.R.B." column, caused a shaking of hoary heads when he declared his reaction to "Iranamok" as "Ho ho ho." These days, *TNR* is a house of talents, frequently divided against itself, and all the livelier as a result. Leon Wieseltier, who moonlights for *Vanity Fair,* is literary editor, and the back pages contain the best book reviews published in America outside the *New York Review of Books*. Like Henry Villard's *Nation* in the nineteenth century, or like *Ramparts, NYR, Rolling Stone,* and *Esquire* in the sixties and early seventies, *TNR* is indispensable and unignorable.

Second best is the *Nation*. Since 1865 the *Nation,* "a weekly journal devoted to Politics, Literature, Science and Art," has published six thousand issues. Its contributors have ranged from Francis Parkman and Henry James to Leon Trotsky, Bertrand Russell, André Malraux, James

Agee, and I. F. Stone, and among the poets, Yeats, Auden, and Frost. The *Nation* was conceived by the journalist E. L. Godkin, the Harvard scholar Charles Eliot Norton, and the architect Frederick Law Olmsted, who designed Central Park. It was said of Oswald Garrison Villard, editor from 1918 to 1932, that he "made more acres of public men acutely miserable per unit of circulation, than any other editor alive."

The present incumbent, Victor Navasky (author of *Kennedy Justice* and other books), is one of the most highly regarded editors in the business, and he too knows how to afflict the comfortable and the elected. The *Nation*'s critics, correspondents, and regular contributors include Arthur C. Danto, Christopher Hitchens, Terence Rafferty, Andrew Kopkind, Calvin Trillin, and Alexander Cockburn. Gore Vidal is a contributing editor. The *Nation* has been immune to the virus of neoconservatism, and it has never been susceptible to conventional wisdom. A recent lead article, for example, questioned what is accomplished by draconian penalties for drunk drivers ("Getting MADD in Vain"). The *Nation* lacks *TNR*'s dandyish ease, preferring honest indignation at the administration's latest enormity. On the other hand, Calvin Trillin is one of the funniest writers around, and a satirical article about the Left's sentimental attachment to folksinging brought in as much mail as the Iran-Contra affair. "Teenagers in Managua are breakdancing on street corners . . . so who do leftists send as cultural ambassadors? Peter, Paul and Mary, with songs about dead flowers," wrote indignant reader Sara Miles of New York City.

How many other 120-year-olds do you know who are still raising hell?

King Named Henry

The lion in winter

BEST known, and still good copy after four hundred years, is Henry VIII. However, Henry IV of France (1553–1610), known as Henry of Navarre, and Henry II of England (1133–89) were greater kings and equally vivid personalities. In recent years, Henry II has even given the old bigamist a run for his money as the subject of popular plays and films. Henry VIII has been portrayed by Charles Laughton (*Loves of Henry VIII*), Richard Burton (*Anne of a Thousand Days*), and Robert Shaw (*A Man for All Seasons*); Henry II by Peter O'Toole (twice: first as a young king in *Becket* and then as an old man in *The Lion in Winter*)—though it is for other reasons that he receives our nomination for second best.

Henry II was obliged to invade England to claim his birthright from King Stephen, and thereafter succeeded in founding the Plantagenet dynasty. In addition to England, he ruled half of France. He was a shrewd and tireless administrator, and revolutionized English jurisprudence. The appointment of his friend Thomas à Becket as archbishop of Canterbury turned out to be a notably bad move in his battle with clerical privilege and was highly damaging to his historical reputation. He is popularly blamed for Becket's assassination at the altar of Canterbury Cathedral, having apparently invited more than a rhetorical answer to his famous exasperated question, "Who will rid me of this turbulent priest?"

Similarly dramatic was his marriage to the willful and cultivated Eleanor of Aquitaine. The ungrateful bride later supported her sons in a revolt against Henry in 1173, for which he had her confined for thirteen years. According to legend, she also murdered Henry's lover, "fair Rosamund." Although Henry was one of England's most effective monarchs, and despite the efforts of Peter O'Toole, he is less well known than Becket; Eleanor, a great patroness of the arts; or his sons, Richard the Lion-Hearted and Prince John.

As for best, we'll have to go with Henry IV of France, convert to Catholicism ("Paris is worth a mass"), patron of industry, brave soldier, and the most popular of all the kings of France. Can fifty million Frenchmen be wrong?

Last Words

Say no more

BACK against the wall, spurning a blindfold, puffing a last cigarette . . . who among us hasn't fantasized facing down a firing squad and going out, like Walter Mitty or (perhaps) Ambrose Bierce, with a bitter quip, a pregnant apothegm, a gallant sentiment? Unfortunately, a firing squad is never around when you need it.

A popular favorite in this category, especially among college sophomores, is from Gertrude Stein (d. 1946). On her deathbed, according to a biographer, she said, "What is the answer?" After a short silence she laughed and added, "In that case, what is the question?"

For runner-up, we nominate the nineteenth-century British prime minister Lord Palmerston (d. 1865) who, in his final illness, proclaimed stoutly: "Die, my dear Doctor?—That's the *last* thing I shall do!"

Pure
Silver

Law of Human Behavior

*A closed mouth
gathers no feet*

MURPHY'S Law ("Anything that can go wrong, will go wrong") raises some intriguing questions. What sort of life must Murphy have led? Certainly he owned an Edsel. And he probably traded it for a British sports car. Possibly he sold his Xerox stock at ten to invest in Nehru jackets. Poor Murph. His one claim to immortality is the legacy of his all-embracing law, certainly one of the best of its genre. Unfortunately, he neglected to append his first name to it, so we shall never know his exact identity.

History is rich with Murphy's antecedents. Shakespeare in particular was fond of formulating variations on the theme. From *King Lear* (with whom Murphy might with good reason claim some kind of kinship) comes:

> The worst is not,
> So long as we can say, "This is the worst."

Other revealed principles tend to deal with more specific areas of human endeavor. British M.P. John Morley is first credited (in 1887) with the observation that "politics is a field where the choice lies constantly between two blunders." Which reminds us that no one who has observed the inner workings of the political process (or visited a slaughterhouse) is unfamiliar with the Sausage Principle: "People who love sausage and respect the law should never watch either being made." Gold's Law of the Marketplace echoes another familiar sentiment: "If the shoe fits, it's ugly," a principle likely to be encountered on the same day as Etorre's observation, "The other line always moves faster."

The Law of Selective Gravity ("An object will always fall so as to do the most damage") is the basis for Jenning's Corollary: "The chance of the bread falling with the buttered side down is directly proportional to the cost of the carpet." These principles of science naturally lead us to a basic law of academic research (which can be universally applied to federally funded projects and research that leads to an advanced degree): Gordon's Law, which states, "If a research project is not worth doing at all, it is not worth doing well." But the researcher, of course, can always blame the Golden Rule of Arts and Sciences: "Whoever has the gold makes the rules." And then there is Denniston's Rule (though we have also heard it attributed to Oscar Wilde), which strikes us as an apt judgment upon those condemned to the Nautilus room of the Family Fitness Center: "Virtue is its own punishment."

Surely of these, Murphy's Law, if only by virtue of its universal application, is the best. Second best honors, therefore, must go to O'Toole, whose precise formulation of his commentary on Murphy's Law reveals a wit no less perceptive: "Murphy was an optimist."

For further study of the principles that guide us as we stumble through God's big practical joke (don't tell us Job wouldn't have appreciated a little humor now and then), we recommend Arthur Bloch's *Murphy's Law—And Other Reasons Why Things Go Wrong* and *Murphy's Law, Book Two: More Reasons Why Things Go Wrong*.

Law
School

Less is more

THE best law school to graduate from is precisely the one you think it is: Harvard. The faculty is stellar, the library is the biggest, the pool of scholarship money is immense (this is a university that's been collecting interest on its massive endowment for three hundred years), and it's *Harvard,* for God's sake, which enhances your chances of graduating and walking into a job as, say, secretary of state.

The second best law school is no surprise, either: Yale. What *is* surprising is the difference between these two ivy-covered institutions. Harvard is immense; with nearly 1,800 students, it's the biggest *real* law school in the U.S. (There are a few bigger ones, but their application forms are printed on matchbook covers.) Yale's enrollment is a third of Harvard's, and its student-faculty ratio (11–1) is also less than half that of its older, larger rival (24–1). That means that your chance of actually getting to *know* your professors is better than twice as good at Yale.

You want selectivity? Yalies' median LSAT score is 44 out of a possible 48; their median undergrad GPA is 3.77. Harvard doesn't release these figures, which means (we suspect) that they're fractionally lower than Yale's. What we *do* know is that Yale accepts eleven percent of its applicants; Harvard accepts twelve percent.

Let's not quibble about statistics, though. Both student bodies are smart. Both schools cost about the same amount of money per year: $17,000-plus. And graduates of both places stand a very low chance of ending up on the unemployment line. Law review editors breeze into those $65,000-a-year Wall Street jobs, and everyone else who wants one gets a nice job with an office in a good private firm. This is an undeniable advantage in these days of the lawyer glut and the even worse law-student glut. As recently as fifteen years ago, a graduate of a decent law school could be assured of a job practicing law. This is no longer the case.

The real difference between Yale and Harvard is not who gets in or what happens to them after they get out. The real difference is in what the students experience while they're *there*. Although Yale offers fewer courses than Harvard, Yale students don't have a set curriculum beyond *first term*. What's more, that first term is graded pass-fail. Law review membership is open to anyone who writes a publishable note, and it's not as crucial to future employment as it is at most schools, because Yale releases no information about its grading curve; nobody (including you) knows your class ranking.

How does student life at Yale compare to that at Harvard? The difference is very much the difference between a large institution and a small one. Life at Harvard is much as you've read about in *One L* and seen on *The Paper Chase*. There's a lot of pressure, especially during the first year, and it can seem a big, impersonal place. Yale is looser, more relaxed—almost more intimate, if "intimate" is an adjective that can ever be properly applied to such a thing as a law school. If these are the qualities that attract you, then it's Harvard that's second best.

Pure Silver

Literary
Anecdote

"Somebody's boring me"

THERE are no authentic anecdotes about Shakespeare, at least none that we know to be authentic, but there is a persistent rumor about a groupie who hung around the stage door at the Globe and eventually got up the courage to invite the actor Richard Burbage, who was playing Richard III, to come up and see her sometime.

According to John Aubrey's *Lives of Eminent Men,* "Shakespeare overhearing their conclusion went before, was entertained, and at his game ere Burbage came. Then message being brought that Richard the Third was at the door, Shakespeare caused return to be made that William the Conqueror was before Richard the Third." A likely story.

Our favorite, and the connoisseur's choice for best, concerns Gérard de Nerval, a French writer who lived in the first half of the nineteenth century. A proto-symbolist and precursor of the surrealists, Nerval was a notorious eccentric. In his later years, he was once seen leading a lobster on a blue ribbon through the gardens of the Palais Royal. When a solicitous passerby inquired about his odd choice of a pet, the poet replied gravely that a lobster never barked at one, and moreover it "knows the secrets of the deep." Another of Nerval's eccentricities was displaying an old apron string, which he claimed was the garter of the Queen of Sheba. (At other times, he said it had belonged to Madame de Maintenon.) Eventually, he hanged himself with it.

C. P. Smith's *Annals of the Poets* is a treasury of the eccentricities, foibles, and aberrations of the English poets. John Milton, for example, was vain about his looks. "In the controversy with Morus, the latter did not scruple to charge Milton with physical ugliness and to emphasize especially the condition of his eyes, then going blind . . . And Milton did not hesitate to answer bad taste in kind. He issued a public declaration of his good looks, stating particularly that his eyes were 'externally un-injured. They shine with an unclouded light, just like the eyes of one whose vision is perfect.' "

Wordsworth was another sublime egotist. A contemporary diarist records that at dinner at Leigh Hunt's, Coleridge was to be heard quoting Wordsworth, and so was Wordsworth. At another party in London, the host produced a watch that had belonged to Milton. "All the guests crowded around to have a look except Wordsworth, who stood apart alone and taking out his own watch held it long in his hand, gazing at it in silent reverence."

William Blake prided himself on his spiritual contact with various heavenly personages. When the engraver Fuseli remarked that one of Blake's drawings must have won him a compliment, the poet replied that, yes, the Virgin Mary liked it very much. In turn, Fuseli remarked that, obviously, her taste was not *always* immaculate.

Irish writers figure in the liveliest anecdotes from modern times—Oscar Wilde turns up in so many he deserves a category to himself. Oliver St. John Gogarty, for example, was a celebrated surgeon and a senator in the Irish parliament. He barely escaped an IRA firing squad by "pleading a natural necessity" and then diving into the river Liffey. What assured him immortality was being the model for stately, plump Buck Mulligan in his ex-friend James Joyce's novel *Ulysses*. Gogarty spent his later years in New York, and a friend remembered him telling a story one night at a Third Avenue bar.

"And when he was about to come to the point, a young man sitting by the bar went over and placed a coin in a jukebox. All hell broke loose. The expression on Gogarty's face changed; he became very sad, a combination of sadness and anger, and he said, 'Oh dear God in Heaven, that I should find myself thousands of miles from home, an old man at the mercy of every retarded son of a bitch who has a nickel to drop in that bloody illuminated coal-scuttle.' "

Joyce had a morbid fear of dogs, and when out walking was reported to keep his pockets filled with stones, in order that he might better scare them away. On the other hand, he was a fearless literary critic. "You are too old for me to help you," he announced to W. B. Yeats when, as a raw youth of twenty, he was introduced to the great man. (Yeats was then thirty-seven.) Unshaken by Joyce's bad manners, the poet recognized his genius, but could not help remarking to friends, "Never have I seen so much pretension with so little to show for it."

Years later, when he had become world famous, Joyce was approached by a young man in Zurich who asked, "May I kiss the hand that wrote *Ulysses*?"

"No," said Joyce. "It did lots of other things too."

The British biographer Lytton Strachey was an early, discreet exponent of gay lib. He was also theatrically epicene with a falsetto voice and a pacifist. In the First World War, he declared himself a conscientious objector and was summoned to appear before a military tribunal.

"I understand, Mr. Strachey, that you have a conscientious objection to war?" the chairman demanded.

"Oh no, not at all," Strachey squeaked, "only to this war."

"Tell me, Mr. Strachey, what would you do if you saw a German soldier trying to violate your sister?" (We are told this stock question "previously never failed to embarrass the claimant.")

Strachey considered, and at last replied with a grave air: "I should try to interpose my body between them." (Both of these stories are retold in the excellent, though somewhat unadventurous, *Oxford Book of Literary Anecdotes.*)

But back to the Irish. For second best we nominate Rayner Heppenstall's recollection of a morning he spent with Dylan Thomas in a sunny field near Newlyn.

"Dylan was carrying around with him and intermittently sipping from a flagon of 'champagne wine tonic,' a Penzance herbalist's highly intoxicating brew sold very cheaply and without license. Dylan talked copiously, then stopped.

" 'Somebody's boring me,' he said. 'I think it's me.' "

Loser

*Snatching defeat from
the jaws of victory*

No area of human endeavor has consistently provided such spectacular opportunities for the demonstration of incompetence and stupidity as that of warfare. But even amidst the crowded field of bunglers that have risen up with each generation, century after century, to lead whoever will follow into pointless death, one man stands out as a loser among losers.

It is a miracle that the Confederacy lost the Civil War with Major General Ambrose Everett Burnside fighting for the North. No tactical or numerical advantage was so great that Burnside couldn't dispose of it in battle along with a considerable number of his troops.

At the beginning of the Battle of Antietam, Burnside's forces vastly outnumbered those of his enemy. But that was before "Burn" (an ominous sobriquet) ordered his troops to cross a narrow bridge in single file within close range of the Southerners. *After* his soldiers were thus decimated, he learned that the creek below the bridge was only a couple of feet deep and could easily have been forded with little or no danger.

Burnside's loony tactics grew stranger as the war progressed. At one point it seemed as if he were finally on the verge of winning a major engagement. He had the enemy bottled up; they were running low on ammunition. Victory seemed certain. Then Burnside had one of those astonishing inspirations that filled his staff with panic (those who had managed thus far to survive). He had a tunnel dug beneath the enemy forces and ordered it filled with dynamite. His plan was to have his troops rush through the trench created by the explosion and leap out upon the enemy in the middle of their own camp.

At the moment of detonation, vast clouds of dirt and debris burst into the air, and the Union soldiers dashed forward through the narrow cleft. Unfortunately, the trench proved to be too deep, and when the dust settled moments later, the Confederate forces were astounded to discover they now surrounded Burnside's troops, who were helplessly trapped in a pit. President Lincoln was not overly surprised by the news. "Only Burnside could have managed such a coup," he said, "wringing one last spectacular defeat from the jaws of victory."

For second best (only because he killed fewer of his own men) we nominate General Antonio López de Santa Anna of Mexico, who lost every battle he ever fought during the Mexican-American War. His one claim to victory was the defeat of the Alamo during the Texas Revolution, in which the 180 defenders were eventually overwhelmed by Santa Anna's force of several thousand. Unfortunately for the Mexican general, however, the fall of the Alamo galvanized support for the Texan secessionists who, in a display of hitherto unachieved unanimity, went on to win the war.

Loser

But it was during a battle with the French in the 1830s that Santa Anna first displayed the unique quality of his military genius. He tried to launch a surprise attack on his enemy by dressing his own soldiers in French uniforms. Unfortunately for Santa Anna, the French had a deeper appreciation of Gallic military apparel than he did. They had little trouble distinguishing their own nattily attired troops from their improperly turned-out opponents. The Mexicans, however, were unable to tell the difference between the enemy and their own forces, and, after some initial confusion, the French discreetly withdrew and simply allowed the Mexicans to kill each other.

While fighting the Texans in 1836, Santa Anna established a camp near a woods where he knew the enemy was hiding. Demonstrating serene confidence in the superiority of his forces, he ordered his troops to take their afternoon siesta. It took the Texans less than eighteen minutes to overrun the Mexicans. Santa Anna reportedly slept through the entire battle.

Martini

Unsubtle assault

M. F. K. Fisher once confessed, "A well-made dry martini or Gibson, correctly chilled and nicely served, has been more often my true friend than any two-legged creature. . . . It, like other more subtle assaults upon our senses, can bring peace with the pain, and a kind of surcease, gastronomical and therefore spiritual, from the world's immediate anguish."

Now, then: a martini is made with gin, not vodka. It is stirred, not shaken. (Ian Fleming certainly got that all wrong.) And it includes vermouth. Fetishists of the cinder-dry martini who merely wave a vermouth bottle in the general vicinity, are drinking straight gin, like Mrs.

Gamp in the Dickens novel. Nonetheless, restraint is in order; FDR, a famous martini man, made his so vermouthy that "they looked like varnish!" an appalled witness confided.

Martinis should be drunk only as an aperitif, and in moderation. They always taste better in bars and bistros. And the only place a proper martini belongs is in the classic funnel-shaped glass. (Even though they carry M. F. K.'s imprimatur, we cannot endorse so-called champagne glasses or wine goblets.) The rim of the glass should be rubbed with lemon peel, and then either the twisted peel or a green olive plopped in. (For a Gibson, substitute two pearl onions: they commemorate the most famous features of the Gibson Girl.) No ice. A proper martini is always served "up."

No other cocktail has inspired a cult to equal the martini's, or touched off so many fervent controversies, or associated itself so tenaciously with wit, urbanity, and cozy afternoons in wood-paneled barrooms—as in the quip, attributed by some to Robert Benchley, by others to Alexander Woollcott, "I've got to get out of these wet clothes and into a dry martini." (Apropos, it's an article of faith in San Francisco that the cocktail was invented by an inspired bartender in nearby Martinez, in the days when travelers required weatherproofing for the ferry trip across the Bay.)

One of the better martinis to be found in the Bay Area today is served at the Santa Fe in Berkeley, where master chef Jeremiah Tower has concocted a "perfect" martini (Boodle's gin, drop of gold Herradura tequila, twist of lime). It was inevitable that someone would come up with a Cajun martini. Here's *Esquire*'s version: decant a fifth of gin or vodka into a big jelly jar along with one red and two green jalapeño peppers (the latter split lengthwise and deveined), and stash for a day or two in the fridge. Serve over ice in old-fashioned glasses. Provocative, but such novelties will never replace the best martini, which consists, in Robert Benchley's immortal formulation, of three parts gin (we prefer

Beefeater's with its tangy herbals) and enough vermouth to take away that ghastly watery look.

But if you want to commit heresy, what better recipe to follow than that of Spanish director Luis Buñuel, who did everything wrong, but with the same panache he displays in such classic films as *Viridiana* and *The Discreet Charm of the Bourgeoisie*? His formula, our second best martini, appears in his autobiography, *My Last Sigh*, and only the most hidebound purist could resist it.

"The day before your guests arrive, put all the ingredients—glasses, gin, and shaker—in the refrigerator. Use a thermometer to make sure the ice is about twenty degrees below zero (centigrade). Don't take anything out until your friends arrive; then pour a few drops of Noilly Prat and half a demitasse spoon of Angostura bitters over the ice. Shake it, then pour it out, keeping only the ice, which retains a faint taste of both. Then pour straight gin over the ice, shake it again and serve."

Buñuel said the dry martini played a "primordial role" in his life. And consider, he lived to be eighty-three.

Mexican Beach Resort

Another lousy sunset in paradise

"BEACHES are the same the world over," says Wright Morris in his novel *Love among the Cannibals*. "You peel down and then you peel off; they serve you up raw meat, dark meat, or flesh nicely basted in olive oil. A strip of sun and sand where the sex is alert and the mind is numb." Of course, there are *some* differences you can detect even behind a pair of Ray-Bans.

In Mexico, for example, Acapulco has been colonized by the Concorde set, with the result that lunch costs as much as it does in Cannes. Cancún, on the Yucatán peninsula, is almost as pricey. Both are world-class resorts that feature first-class service every step of the way from bed to beach (and back). But also throbbing with that sensual music are Puerto Vallarta and Ixtapa—two sensibly priced Pacific resorts that amply demonstrate our contention that second best is sometimes better.

Back in the sixties, Puerto Vallarta was still your basic paradigmatic sleepy fishing village when destiny (and MGM) arrived in the form of the cast and crew of *Night of the Iguana*, directed by John Huston and starring Richard Burton and Ava Gardner. Since Burton was accompanied by his bride, Elizabeth Taylor Wilding Todd Fisher, the invasion was joined by a large percentage of the world press. Things have not been the same since, old-timers dreamily maintain; the astonishment is that Puerto Vallarta has somehow managed to save its raffish old soul.

One of the nicest things about Puerto Vallarta is the availability of inexpensive accommodations in the heart of the village. Of course, there are the big beach hotels: a Holiday Inn, a Sheraton, and a Fiesta America. But for old New World ambience, we recommend the Oceano. Built pre-Burton, it has been refurbished to provide post-Burton comforts (though it's the atmospherics, not the comforts, that are lavish). Likewise, the Hotel Los Cuatro Vientos, which stands as another whitewashed, red-tiled relic of earlier, less hectic days.

Just south of town, where the jungle tumbles down the steep hillsides to the sea, the Tomatlán River offers freshwater bathing in crystal-clear pools among giant boulders and waterfalls. The trail to the pools—through a botanist's dreamscape—is now paved, and ends at a thatch-roofed bar-restaurant complex overlooking the river.

Like costlier Cancún, our second second best, Ixtapa, is the creation of the relentless developers at FONATUR, Mexico's National Trust Fund for the Promotion of Tourism. Ixtapa is just far enough away from Acapulco (150 miles to the north) to have retained its charm and natural beauty. Best of all, it's located right next to the sixteenth-century port of Zihuantanejo, a pleasant, cobblestoned village nestled on green hillsides around a pristine bay.

Ixtapa's developers have thoughtfully included an eighteen-hole

Robert Trent Jones golf course (to which the rumored threat of alligators has given a nice edge to the term "water hazard"), in addition to what many visitors consider the most beautiful hotel in Mexico. Each of the Hotel Camino Real's 450 rooms is spacious and well-furnished, including hammocks and chaise longues on the westward-facing terraces. However, like the other first-class hotels in Ixtapa—including a Sheraton, a Hotel Inn, and a Dorado Pacifico—prices are at the top of the scale. More moderately priced are the El Presidente and the Riviera del Sol.

In addition to golf, there's tennis and, of course, water sports: deep-sea fishing, scuba diving, snorkeling, waterskiing, windsurfing, sailing, and even parasailing.

We haven't mentioned specific prices because of the current (i.e., perennially) unstable nature of the Mexican economy. As we write, the peso has never been a better bargain. However, the Mexican government periodically adjusts the hotel rates.

Newspaper in the World

Salmon pink hauteur

PRAVDA has a circulation of ten million. That fact alone establishes it as the single most influential newspaper in the world. The *New York Times* (circulation 900,000) is frequently cited as the ideological counterpart of *Pravda* and the closest thing this country has to a national newspaper (we're not holding our breath waiting for *USA Today* to come up to that standard), but many Europeans complain both papers are biased, provincial, and even naive in their coverage of world affairs. *The Times* and *The Guardian* of London, although discouraged by Britain's strict libel laws from doing much investigative reporting, provide a more balanced view of world events (at least in terms of column inches), and *Die Welt, Le Monde*, and the *Neue Zuercher Zeitung* are similarly cosmopolitan papers that are highly rated for their evenhanded and thoughtful coverage of planetary affairs.

These are the papers that best reflect the prevailing cultural and political climates of the societies they represent, and do much to shape a popular view of the world. But they are not enough for the world's power brokers who require a reliable supra-national guide to the daily functioning of the planet's political and economic machinery. That is why they supplement their reading with the salmon pink pages of the *Financial Times* of London, our nomination for second best.

The *FT*'s daily circulation of 250,000 copies is distributed to 156 countries, and it is considered *must* reading by anyone involved in international financial affairs. The *FT*'s contacts in the world of high finance are legendary. Saudi Arabia's former oil minister, Sheikh Ahmed Yamani, once held up a press conference because the *FT*'s Middle East reporter was missing. "Where is Richard Johns?" Yamani said after surveying the crowd of reporters in a Geneva hotel conference room. "We cannot begin without him." They didn't.

Johns eventually developed such a strong rapport with Yamani that he ceased going to the OPEC press conferences altogether. He simply waited in his hotel room for the sheikh to drop by, and together they would thrash out Saudi Arabia's oil strategy.

When the Shah of Iran, disgusted with the *FT*'s persistent policy of referring to the Arabian Gulf as the Arabian Gulf (instead of the Persian Gulf), ordered Iranian advertisers not to pay their bills, the *Financial Times* editor, Gordon Newton, responded with typical *FT* hauteur. "This Shah of Iran," he said, "who does he think he is?"

More recently, the *FT* was the first to report the significance of the collapse of the Penn Square Bank of Oklahoma. It was weeks before the *Wall Street Journal* realized the import of the event. By the time American papers were just beginning to realize that the bank's collapse might be having adverse effects on more than just a handful of Oklahoma farmers, the *FT* had already run twenty-six stories, including analyses of how Penn Square's failure had destabilized the international market for U.S. Eurobonds.

But while it has built its reputation upon its uncanny perception of economic affairs, the *FT* is equally astute in covering hard news. Perhaps the only drawback to the *FT* is its unstinting demand on the reader. Reporters are enjoined from reducing the complexity of world events to the usual journalistic clichés. But while this may restrict its circulation among the masses, it has enhanced the paper's reputation among discerning readers. "They do an excellent job," says Malcolm Forbes, who should know. And it has a splendid crossword puzzle.

Olive Oil

Athena's oil

IN Greek mythology, olive oil was the gift of the goddess Athena. The distinction between people who cook with olive oil and those who cook with butter is as basic as the distinction between whiskey and wine cultures, mushroom gatherers and nonmushroom gatherers, north and south, Latins and Celts. Today, the most famous varieties of *ollio del olivas* are pressed in Italy (known to the ancients in Pericles' time as "Magna Graecia"), but the best, in our estimation, comes from Modesto, California.

As the label says, "Sciabica's (pronounced Sha-bee-ka's) brand is different. The finest olive oil made, Sciabica's is "A 100% PURE VIR-

GIN UNREFINED NATURAL CALIFORNIA OLIVE OIL, a true quality food which is still COLD PRESSED the old-fashioned way so as to retain its natural color, aroma, and flavor, assuring your food dollar's full value with a full natural olive oil." Moreover, Sciabica's is the only varietal olive-oil presser in the world, using Mission, Manzanillo, and Marsala varieties. It's pricey (upwards of six dollars for a 375-milliliter bottle), and in most cities you have to hunt for it in a natural foods store.

Pure Silver

About second best, we found surprising agreement among chefs. While some might dispute our rating of Sciabica's, preferring exotic extra-virginal oils from obscure Italian exporters, everybody's number two was Olio Sasso from Lucca—fresh, fruity, dependable, and cheap, available in cans and bottle.

Opera from Wagner's *Ring* Cycle

The short of it

CLOCKING in at eighteen hours spread out over four evenings, Richard Wagner's *Ring of the Nibelungen* allows ample time to repair to the opera bar and argue out the claims for best and second best operas of the cycle. Opinion is about equally divided between *Die Walküre*, the second part of the tetralogy, and the final opera, *Die Götterdämmerung*. While it must be admitted that the latter has much of the work's most glorious music (the Brunhild/Siegfried love duet, the titanic Immolation Scene), partisans of *Die Walküre* insist it is the most human part of Wagner's uncompromisingly mythological masterwork, containing as it does such familiar conflicts as brother versus sister, husband versus wife, father versus son, and father versus daughter. Its supporters also point to *its* musical wonders: Siegfried's Rhine Journey and the Siegfried Funeral Music must be the best and second best pieces written for the express purpose of allowing stage-hands to change the sets.

But if *Die Walküre* and *Die Götterdämmerung* may be said to be tied for first place, what is second best? *Siegfried* may be quickly disposed of. The trouble with *Siegfried* is, in a word, Siegfried. This portrayal of youthful innocence usually comes off as middle-aged loutishness bordering dangerously on mental retardation. It seems to take Siegfried forever to figure out the simplest things: that the dwarf Mime is obviously not dear old Dad; that there are *two* sexes. (Siegfried, never having seen a woman before entering Brunhild's ring of fire, exclaims "That is no man!"—thereby delivering one of the most surefire unintentional laugh-lines in opera.)

This leaves us with *Das Rheingold*, the first opera of the cycle, as second best. True, it is something of a Wagnerian bagatelle, being a mere two-hour-forty-five-minute one-act prologue, and musically it is the most primitive, beginning with over 136 bars of the chord E-flat major rising to a crescendo, but then this primitive quality is a proper aural equivalent of its subject—nothing less than the beginning of the world.

Das Rheingold is also packed with incident, recounting how the evil dwarf Alberich steals the sacred Rhine gold from the Rhine maidens, only to lose it to Wotan, who loses it to the giants Fafner and Fasolt. It is a story subject to a bewildering variety of interpretations. To George Bernard Shaw it was a Marxist indictment of the Industrial Revolution; to others it is a grim Schopenhauerian parable of man's useless tragic struggle; to the Freudians (more spiritedly) it depicts the thwarting of primal gratification in which love is renounced in favor of power, domination, and riches.

There are as many musical thrills as there are potent dramatic confrontations in *Das Rheingold*: the thunderous entrance of the giants;

Alberich's eerily evil hymn to greed; and Donner's tremendous thunderclap, which clears the clouds and produces a rainbow bridge over which the gods must cross to the strains of a pompous, triumphant *bolero* tune in order to enter their new home. It must also be noted that until recently *Das Rheingold* was as accident-prone as the other operas of the *Ring*. In the 1930s, the illusion of the Rhine Maidens swimming in the depths of the Rhine was created by having three ladies float about on piano wires like plump Peter Pans. But in one performance a few crossed wires produced a literal head-on collision, leaving two unconscious Rhine maidens wafting in midair while the remaining, conscious one was obliged to sing all three roles. Finally, the two limp ladies were unceremoniously yanked off the stage into the wings, beyond the horrified gaze of the audience.

For its dramatic incident and the sheer number of its interesting characters (not to mention its brevity), we nominate *Das Rheingold* as second best.

Party School

Toga, toga, toga!

In this category we bow to authority. Despite the fact that the authors have spent a cumulative total of twenty-one years in higher education at eight campuses (which is nothing compared to some people we can name), we recognize Hugh Hefner's investigative journalists as having the final word when it comes to serious partying. In a six-month research project, *Playboy* magazine polled undergraduate "campus club leaders, dorm rush chairmen, fraternity presidents and other campus social lights" at over 250 colleges and universities to determine where partying, including old-fashioned drunkenness and promiscuity, is most intense. The editors strike us as being a mite credulous (some of these stories were circulated at Babylon U. in 1700 B.C.), but all in all, the survey is heartening evidence that not all undergraduates spend their evenings rehearsing for a job interview with Drexel, Burnham.

Tops in depravity is California State University at Chico: "Normal people have moved out of the area because of the partying. 'It's so hot here that it'll make your skin bubble.' " But here again, geography considered, second best is better. At number two University of Miami in glitzy Coral Gables, "students have access to (and can afford) most party refreshments. 'We have sex in hot tubs. Preferably in groups,' " reported one student informant to the wide-eyed inquirer from *Playboy*. The party animals at Chico State have to settle for the Bidwell Lava Pits.

Pasta

Pasta de résistance

IF you're still throwing it at the kitchen wall to see if it's done, then you have not yet crossed over the threshold into the chic new world of *nuova cucina*. Enter and you will discover agnolotti filled with goat cheese and porcini mushrooms, lobster ravioli, and tortelli stuffed with venison. Sauces and fillings of such elegance and delicacy require pasta to match. Those with opportunity, appetite, and discerning taste would as soon put powdered milk in a cup of Blue Mountain as grind their Parmigiano-Reggiano over pasta made with farina.

Pasta Italian style has been around at least since the thirteenth century when invading Mongols first introduced it to Europe. (There's no historical evidence to confirm the legend that Marco Polo brought it back from his travels to China.)

Italian-made pastas are generally superior to American brands. They have a slight nutty flavor, a firmer texture, and generally hold a sauce better. The difference is both in the ingredients and the method of preparation. The Italians use fresh eggs and semolina. Most American manufacturers use dried eggs, and many blend farina into the flour. (That's why the water tends to turn milky when you cook U.S.-made pasta.) The best of the small Italian houses use bronze dies to extrude their products, which gives the finished pasta a rougher texture that holds sauces better. Bigger firms, and virtually all American companies, use Teflon-coated dies which produce a shiny surface so smooth that sauces slide right off, like rain from a slicker.

The best pastas come from the Campania and Abruzzi regions of Italy. Particularly noted among them are Gerardo di Nola, Colavita, Del Verde, and DeCecco (the most widely available). Unfortunately, the Gerardo di Nola, which has a legendary reputation among pastaphiles, is almost impossible to find in this country. The others are generally reliable, but as they have expanded production and modernized their facilities to meet the growing demands of the American and European export markets, the quality of their products has suffered the inevitable consequences.

For second best we recommend Martelli. The only thing wrong with this product line is that it is so limited. Martelli offers only spaghetti, spaghettini, maccheroni, and penne. But this sixty-year-old family business has refused to expand or modernize, relying upon a somewhat slower process to produce a high-quality product consistently. Its carefully selected blend of durum is locally ground for freshness. And the Martellis mix and knead their dough for thirty to forty minutes (that's almost twice as long as other manufacturers), which they say improves the flavor. Finally, they use only bronze dies to squeeze out the pasta shapes, ensuring a truly sauce-grabbing product.

Peanut
Butter
in a Jar

Not a pretty sight

ELSEWHERE in the world, such as West Africa and Indonesia, pureed peanuts (the peanut is a legume, incidentally, not a nut) are used to sauce fowl and other meats, and to our mind the very best use of peanut butter is the incandescent *satay* sauce of Java. In the United States, however, research indicates that the most avid consumers of peanut butter are six- to eight-year-olds living in the Midwest, and they would likely think as little of saffron chicken with peanut-butter sauce as an Indonesian would dream of peanut-butter-and-jelly sandwiches.

Not that peanut butter is entirely without adult fans over here, though unlike kids, adults tend to prefer the chunky variety. Jif and Skippy's, both available in smooth and crunchy, account between them for nearly fifty percent of sales. The polemicist William F. Buckley, Jr., once confessed himself a Skippy's fan and shared this sentiment with poetry lovers:

> I know that I shall never see
> A poem lovely as Skippy's Peanut Butter.

However, as he explains in his next-to-latest memoir, *Overdrive*, he has apostatized and now prefers Red Wing. "It is quite simply incomparable. Charlton Heston, who had sent me a jar of his favorite stuff, just plain surrendered when I introduced him to Red Wing." Red Wing has a fresh consistency and a nice crunch. It can be difficult to find under its own name, but is available under the house labels of various national chains. Look for the distinctive yellow plastic screw-on cover.

"Old-fashioned" peanut butter is composed of crushed peanuts and, usually, a pinch of salt. Some of the most aggressively "natural" brands, such as Westbrae's, are available unsalted. "Regular" brands are manufactured from blanched peanuts, sweeteners (usually sugar), salt, and hydrogenated fat, i.e., vegetable shortening. The old-fashioned varieties will separate, leaving a pool of peanut oil at the top of the jar. Not a pretty sight—but then, eating a hydrogenated-fat-and-jelly sandwich isn't a pretty thought, either.

Having studied the results of several professional taste tests, we decided as usual to consult our own preferences. If you are a child, you will prefer smooth peanut butter, in which case your first choice would be Neiman Marcus's house brand, with its nice consistency. Since Mom and Dad probably won't spring for it (and you won't be reading this book anyway), settle for second best—much less expensive (Mom and Dad will like that) Jif Creamy.

Now for the rest of us. Like Mr. Buckley (and we rejoice, for once, to discover some common ground with him), we find breakfast without peanut butter on toast incomplete. Yet we find Red Wing a trifle bland, and Chunky Westbrae, which is nothing but crunchy, organic, no-salt peanuts (and hence our choice for best) may be too formidable for some. Just as we thought we'd never find a satisfying second best, R. W. Knudsen produced its "Natural No-Salt-Added Crunchy" peanut butter. It's less grainy than Westbrae's, it smells like the peanuts that vendors sell in ballparks when the boys of summer are playing, and, frankly, we find ourselves hoping the health-food store will run out of Westbrae's so we can buy Knudsen's instead.

Pepper Vodka

Hot stuff

TRUMAN Capote first popularized pepper vodka as an accessory of the cognoscenti in "Mojave," a chapter from his unfinished novel *Answered Prayers*, where it was mentioned with the casual air reserved for only the most exotic indulgences. Stolichnaya's Petrovska is the best pepper vodka. Its reddish tint is not deceptive. It is breathtakingly hot and spicy, and, taken straight up in a frosted liqueur glass, not for the faint-hearted. No additional ingredients are required when mixing Petrovska with tomato juice to make an exquisite Bloody Mary.

Unfortunately, Stolichnaya is Russian. As such, it is subject to the troubled currents of international politics. During the boycott of the 1980 Olympic games, Russian products were, by popular demand, banished from the shelves of American liquor stores. Cases of Stoli were dumped into the harbors of Eastern seaports, and in the minds of its devoted fans, the Bloody Marys served in the best bars took on a wartime ersatz quality and were imbibed with the kind of stoic pride reminiscent of the volunteer rationing of the forties.

Fortunately, neutral Sweden, source of those magnificently engineered Saabs and Volvos and the cheerful, life-affirming films of Ingmar Bergman, now generates a steady supply of pepper vodka to the land of the free. Since 1985, Absolut has been manufacturing an acceptable substitute for Petrovska. True, it lacks the fiery bite of its Russian competitor, but that can be an advantage when it's served undiluted. It is also less expensive than Stoli's pepper vodka, but no less chic.

Pickle

*A fine state for a
cucumber to be in*

BEST are pickles plucked from briny barrels—preferably located on the Lower East Side of Manhattan. Our taste runs to garlicky kosher dills, but we're ecumenical in this regard.

Among the store-bought second best, we recommend Westbrae's ferociously natural garlic-and-pepper home dills (available at health-food stores).

Pocketknife

Mac the Wrench

WITH sixteen blades, twenty-four tools (including a cheese grater), and weighing in at 160 grams, the Victorinox Champion, better known as the Swiss Army knife, is indisputably the finest pocketknife in the world. Lyndon Johnson ordered four thousand embossed with the presidential seal to give to his best friends at his inauguration. Ronald Reagan ordered a more conservative two thousand. When U-2 pilot Francis Gary Powers was shot down over the Soviet Union, he was carrying the usual CIA pocket paraphernalia that included gold coins, secret codes, poison needle, and (what else?) a Swiss Army knife. The slimmer Master Craftsman model is such a marvel of compactness and practicality that NASA made it the official pocketknife for the Skylab and Space Shuttle programs. And, highest accolade of all, the Museum of Modern Art includes the Champion in its collection of well-designed functional objects.

But because Victorinox has a tough time filling all its orders, it has subcontracted the small Swiss firm of Wenger S. A. to help out. Wenger uses the same high-quality French stainless steel and the same standards to produce an identical product.

But Wenger also produces its own knife, priced slightly below the Victorinox Champion but equally well made. It is not, of course, THE Swiss Army knife. Ronald Reagan does not own one. NASA has no plans to send it to Mars. But the second best Wenger has a *wrench*, and the Swiss Army knife does not. So there.

Political Columnist

Dr. Will . . .

. . . **I**s second best. The best political columnist in America is Murray Kempton, when he chooses to write about politics. We imagine George Frederick Will would concur in this judgment, since he ranks Kempton with the late G. K. Chesterton (d. 1936) and the very late Samuel Johnson (d. 1784) among "the columnists I most admire."

Kempton is a liberal, a onetime police reporter whose commentaries combine self-mocking orotundity with colloquial directness—his prose is the objective correlative of a cultivated, unillusioned sensibility that's been around.

In the opinion of some working journalists, second best George Will might have benefited from a few years on the police beat. Son of a philosophy professor, he studied at Trinity College in Connecticut, at Oxford (briefly), and at Princeton, where he took a Ph.D. in political science. After a short spell of teaching at Michigan State (Will describes himself as a "lapsed professor of political philosophy"), he signed on as an aide to an obscure senator and began contributing to William F. Buckley's *National Review*. Thereafter, he divagated into writing columns for the *Washington Post* and *Newsweek* and appearing in various capacities on ABC-TV. Though his celebrity and most of his income are derived from television and lectures, he is certainly the most visible political columnist since Walter Lippmann.

(Walter Lippmann, the late grand panjandrum of columnists, never covered the crime beat, either—but, celebrity aside, other resemblances to Will are few. Lippmann belonged to the legendary Harvard class of 1910, which included T. S. Eliot and John Reed, and in which he shone. As an undergraduate, he was sought out by William James, and his youthful counsel was valued by Theodore Roosevelt and Woodrow Wilson, whom he accompanied to Versailles. He passed through a socialist phase when young. He was a founding editor of *The New Republic* and editorial page editor of the *New York World* before he began writing his celebrated column, "Today and Tomorrow.")

Fame as grand as Will's has pitfalls. He is tender on the subject of his erudition and did not take it kindly when Garry Trudeau invented a "quote boy" to furnish him with the high-flown snippets that are the wonder of his readers. In a display of raw power several presidents would have envied, he forbade his colleague Sam Donaldson even to mention the cartoons on "This Week with David Brinkley." Actually, he isn't a terribly cultivated man, if one may judge from his sparse and philistine comments on art and his jejune play with great names. In a savage review of *The Morning After*, his latest collection of columns, Henry Fairlie lampooned Will's pretensions, concluding, "He rummages among [Western] thought and literature like a bag lady."

It's true, in Will's case a little learning has proved to be not a dangerous but an exceedingly profitable thing (over a million dollars a year). No scholar or deep thinker, he is a highly skilled phrasemaker and publicist. Unlike *New York Times* columnist William Safire, another contender in this category, he rarely comes up with a scoop, preferring to write, in his own description, about "the 'inside' of public matters, not what is secret, but what is latent, the kernel of principle and other significance that exists, recognized or not, 'inside' events, policies and manners."

On the other hand, George Will's columns are *news*. If they are not required reading in the world's chancelleries, as Lippmann's were, they can still crystallize a public mood or disfigure a reputation. E.g., the Vice President's handlers were stunned when Will declared George Bush to be a "lapdog," and presumably there was consternation in the Oval Office when he admitted his friend the President was "slothful."

Though we have other favorites on the op-ed pages, notably Anthony Lewis, Michael Kinsley, and Tom Wicker, this is one of those categories in which vox populi has to be heard, and if Kempton is the profounder observer and the better stylist, Will's unsurpassed combination of influence, quotability, and verve makes him a formidable second best.

Like William Buckley, Gore Vidal, John Kenneth Galbraith—the "literary politicians"—Will has succeeded in crafting a highly salable, trademarkable persona. Less intimidating than the others, he makes a virtue of his ordinariness. What engages the public is precisely the contrast between Milquetoast appearance and brittle self-confidence—between vaulting intellectual pretentions and hoi polloi tastes (McDonald's, afternoons at the ballpark). He has none of Buckley's or Vidal's hauteur. Where his patron Buckley writes books about crossing the Atlantic in a yacht with his grand friends, Will writes columns about going camping with his sons. He is always snappy and epigrammatic; and—another considerable virtue—though operating as a conservative, he exhibits a tonic sense of the contradictions within the movement. For example:

"When conservatives promise to get government 'off the back' of 'the people,' who do they think put it there? . . . Many conservatives insist that America's great problem is just that government is so strong it is stifling freedom. These people call themselves 'libertarian conservatives'—a label a bit like 'promiscuous celibates.' "

Unexpectedly, Will sometimes displays a novelistic flair for character:

"[Strom Thurmond] has Daniel Webster's eyebrows, and eyes like tarnished dimes. He has the large hands and wrists of a man built for seizing and subduing things, as a senator learned when he and Thurmond settled a parliamentary point with a wrestling match."

Will was awarded the Pulitzer Prize for distinguished commentary in 1977. His collections of columns are *The Pursuit of Happiness and Other Sobering Thoughts, The Pursuit of Virtue and Other Tory Notions*, and *The Morning After: American Successes and Excesses 1981–1986*.Nietzsche said, "Many people wait throughout their whole lives for the chance to be good in their own fashion." But lucky George Will elected early on to be a columnist.

Political Consultant

*"All grit and blood
on the floor"*

"THE contest, the winning and losing thing, is big for me," says second best Lee Atwater, the self-confessed "unwashed country boy" whose dream is to see George Bush in the White House. "I can't stand to lose. I'm 28–4 so far, and when I lose I get physically sick. It's right healthy to be a poor loser in this business."

From Aaron Burr to Herbert Hoover, politicians got along nicely without professional political consultants. After all, what did Theodore Roosevelt or his cousin Franklin have to learn from such free-lancers? The oldest modern political-consulting firm, California's Whitaker and Baxter, dates back only to the 1930s.

Yet today, the ascendancy of the consultant is complete. Such penetrating commentators as Sidney Blumenthal of the *Washington Post* believe that the wizards of the media blitz and the direct-mail campaign have replaced the party bosses of yesteryear. As writer David Remnick observes, "Inside the Washington Beltway, consultants such as Pat Caddell, Robert Squier, and Paul Maslin (for Democratic candidates) and Roger Ailes, Ed Rollins, and Jon Deardourff (for Republican candidates) are better known than some senators and most congressmen." Says Larry J. Sabato in his study of the consultant phenomenon, "Gerald Rafshoon's candidate [Jimmy Carter] may have gotten to the White House, but Bailey and Deardourff [Gerald Ford's consultants] were perceived to have won the 1976 presidential contest" because they brought Ford so close from so far behind. Likewise, "Hubert Humphrey lost the 1968 presidential election, but Joseph Napolitan and the Democratic nominee's managers won the blue ribbons from the panel of judges in politics and the press."

Newspapers now nominate "front-running" consultants; moviemakers lionize them. In *The Candidate*, Allen Garfield (playing a rumpled media hotshot said to be modeled on David Garth) helps elect Robert Redford to the Senate. In *Power* ("It's better than sex"), consultant Richard Gere spends as much time in the buff as he does polling.

Following the example of the people who draw up "Best Dressed" lists, we're going to shunt all-time great Garth and his Republican counterpart, Stu Spencer, into a Hall of Fame category all their own. Right now, it's a tight race for top standing between Robert Squier and Lee Atwater . . . and second best, as we said, is Atwater.

Atwater, thirty-seven, cut his teeth campaigning for Strom Thurmond, the Dixiecrat-turned-Republican senator from South Carolina. With Roger Stone (described by *The New Republic* as "The State of the Art Washington Sleazeball"), he is a partner in Campaign Consultants (formerly Black, Manafort, Stone & Atwater). In an *Esquire* profile titled "Why Is Lee Atwater So Hungry?" author Remnick comments, "People in politics say they have not seen anything like Lee Atwater since the days of Huey Long. He may talk of media buys and scientific polling, 'new values,' and 'the coming realignment' . . . but he is all grit, all blood on the floor and don't look back, and you picture him at some political rally, a country fair on a hot summer day, his shirt darkened with lakes of sweat, and he's got one eye on the hecklers and the other on his man, a fat old mountebank in a white suit barking his populist intentions into a microphone."

Atwater's main man, no "fat old mountebank," to be sure, is Vice President George Bush. Indeed, there is talk that if George Bush is inaugurated President in January 1989, Atwater will be his chief of staff.

As a politician, the veep's besetting sin is that of being perceived as "too nice"—this is known in the consulting trade as the "weenie factor." No one has ever accused Harvey Lee Atwater of being too nice. In a 1980 congressional race, he spread the word that his candidate's opponent was mentally unstable. "In college I understand he got hooked up to jumper cables," Atwater allegedly told reporters in an off-the-record briefing.

Why is Atwater, with such credentials, only second best? R. W. Apple, Jr., Washington correspondent for the *New York Times*, describes Squier, who runs the Communications Company in Washington, D.C., as "perhaps the most successful of Democratic campaign consultants." He has been a player in over a hundred campaigns, including work at the highest level for Hubert Humphrey in 1968 and Jimmy Carter in 1976.

In 1986, Squier advised senatorial candidates Terry Sanford, Bob Graham, and Richard Shelby in North Carolina, Florida, and Mississippi, respectively. They won, though all of them had to knock out an incumbent to do so. Atwater's senatorial candidate, Henson Moore in Louisiana, lost. His winners included Carroll Campbell, running for the state house in South Carolina, and congressional hopefuls in North Carolina and Kentucky. Of course, it might be argued that Squier had the better men, but no political consultant worth his bumper stickers would agree that *that* was an insurmountable advantage.

Well, Lee, there's always '88.

Potato
Chip

In the chips

It is said that when faced with death, one's senses are heightened. This may explain why we fervently believe the best potato chip we ever encountered was in the bar at the Ritz Hotel in Paris (now known as the Hemingway Bar), where we had gone in December of 1973 to await the imminent collision of our planet with the comet Kohoutek. No other chip has ever tasted quite so pure, so much like, well, like a fresh potato. So we were pleased to read recently that culinary luminary Craig Claiborne also treasures fond memories of the Ritz chip. But for those of us who find it inconvenient to shop for potato chips in Paris, there's always the second best.

There are, of course, the populist national brands such as Lay's, Granny Goose, and O'Grady's. They'll all do quite nicely, particularly after the first quart of beer. But Pringles is not on our list. Those bland assembly line clones, stamped from dehydrated potato mash, may have captured sixteen percent of the U.S. potato chip market, but the only place we could reasonably imagine serving them is in our fallout shelter two days after we've run out of Spam.

Then there are the smaller firms, for the most part family owned and operated, employing recipes that reflect regional tastes or the eccentricities of somebody's grandfather. The thick, greasy Maui Chips from Hawaii are an inexplicable success in Los Angeles, despite their high cost ($7.95 per 7-ounce bag). Down south there are Zapp's Cajun Craw-Tators that come in several challenging degrees of pepperiness, and up Oregon way, Trader Joe's Habeas Crispus is the local chip of choice. New Englanders have long been enamored of Cape Cod Chips, another greasy maritime product, and in Pennsylvania the straightforward, unadulterated Charles Chip has long competed with our pick for second best.

The Utz family distributes its incomparable product in Virginia, Maryland, and its home state, Pennsylvania, long regarded the spiritual center of the potato chip industry. Utz Chips have been highly rated by *Food & Wine Magazine* and praised by the editors of *Town and Country*. What is their secret? It could be the potatoes themselves (they only use the hardest, roundest, whitest chipping potatoes), or it might be the pure cottonseed oil in which the Utzes fry their chips.

Certainly the speed with which the Utzes get their product to market doesn't hurt. Whatever it is, the giant golden Utz chips are a considerable bargain when you consider how much you save by shopping in Baltimore instead of Paris.

Power Color
for Neckties

Making them see red

According to Audrey Talbot, CEO of Talbot Ties of Carmel-by-the-Sea, purveyor of "club" ties for the Bohemian Club, Stanford University, and Harvard University, the leading power colors are red, burgundy, and yellow, in that order. Yellow is fading away (and it seems only yesterday that a politico couldn't get booked on "Nightline" without one), but burgundy is holding steady as second best. Ten years ago, the order was navy blue, burgundy, and red.

In terms of traditional color symbolism, the wonder is that yellow, which signifies inconstancy or worse, ever edged into the fashion limelight. Blue is the color of hope (thus highly suitable for a political candidate on the hustings), burgundy has some of the regal associations of purple, and red represents the martial virtues. However, it should be noted that wearing a power-colored tie is not guarantee of success. Throughout the 1984 presidential campaign, Walter Mondale wore bright red neckties, and he lost to a man in a brown suit.

Incidentally, Talbot's designers say pink is on its way to becoming the hottest of power colors for ties. But unless you have an application in at *Rolling Stone* or Lucasfilm, or at a very large impersonal corporation owned by your parents, we wouldn't advise wearing one to a job interview.

Projection
Set

The big picture

Iт's taken a while to get the bugs out, but manufacturers are now offering a variety of front- and rear-screen projection TVs that are far superior to the pioneer models of a few years ago. The biggest problems were low image intensity (you had to dim the room lights to see the picture on most early sets), lack of clarity (misaligning the beams caused color blurring that made the image look like a badly printed comic book), and bulkiness (just try fitting a hundred-pound black vinyl cube into *your* furniture scheme). In the current top-of-the-line models, these problems have been minimized and the bulky look pretty much eliminated.

The best (and the biggest) is the Kloss Novabeam Model One-A. The eighteen-inch-high walnut- or oak-veneer projector can pass as an end table, but when you shove it into position and switch it on, it throws a ten-foot (diagonally measured) picture onto your wall. The tuner has 105-channel capability and adapts easily to other sources (such as cable, VCR, or videodisc player). The image is crisp and clear, but the manufacturer recommends you buy the optional six-and-a-half-foot screen for optimum results (without it, you need to dim the room lights). Unfortunately, there's no way to pass off a screen that size as a contemporary Danish sideboard.

Other top designs include Sony, Mitsubishi, and Panasonic. But the second best has most of the features of the top-of-the-line models at a considerably lower price. It also has a few unique innovations that put it (as far as we're concerned) way ahead of the others.

The Sanyo PTV40 is a rear-screen model that doesn't take up much more space than a conventional large-screen set, except that it has a forty-inch screen. It has a lens system that automatically maintains projection alignment, and it puts out a whopping 160 footlamberts. (That's a measure of luminescence, and just to give you an idea, *Consumer Reports* recommends 50 to 80 footlamberts for rear-screen sets.) It has a liquid cooling system that keeps the cathode-ray tube from getting too hot (a main cause of loss of sharpness), an off-air resolution of 320 to 400 lines, a tuner with 140-channel capability, three separate audio/video inputs, built-in stereo circuitry, and a thirty-key infrared remote control.

One final word about Sanyo. It used to be regarded as a kind of Sony clone, producing lower-quality components that were competitive only in terms of price. But that's how Japanese industry got started, remember. Sanyo is now competitive in terms of quality and innovation, and still manages to sell at bargain-basement prices.

Real Estate Deal

Too bad the lawyers from "L.A. Law" weren't around to handle the divorces

When Peter Minuit, acting as an agent for the Dutch West India Company, paid for the twenty-two square miles of Manhattan Island with twenty-four dollars' worth of baubles, he thought he was making the real estate deal of all time. Too bad he bargained with the wrong Indians. The Canarsee tribe, with whom Minuit arranged the purchase, was just passing through and had no real claim to the island. Minuit had to negotiate a new deal with the rightful inhabitants, the Manhattan Indians. Still, the appreciation of real estate values there certainly qualifies the deal as one of the very best, even if the Canarsee had established an unfortunate precedent for real estate brokers.

For second best we elect the deal struck by the Mormon church for Utah. Hounded out of Missouri and Illinois for practicing polygamy, Brigham Young in 1844 led his followers to the arid Salt Lake Valley, then a part of Mexico. But when the Utah Territory was ceded to the U.S. in 1848 at the end of the Mexican-American War, the Mormons again found themselves at odds with the feds. Troops were sent in to quell an anticipated uprising. However, instead of an army of religious zealots, all they found was a peaceful land of shrewd traders who charged so much for supplies that Congress, alarmed by the cost, ordered a withdrawal. But after the Civil War a crusade of former abolitionists led by Harriet Beecher Stowe forced Washington to put new vigor into its efforts to abolish polygamy among the Mormons. The disenfranchised and outlawed Mormon church was driven underground and its members scattered, until in 1890 their leaders agreed, for the survival of the church, to outlaw the practice of polygamy. Congress granted statehood to Utah a few years later.

Today the Mormon church controls a multibillion-dollar empire that includes Beneficial Life Insurance, the Utah-Idaho Sugar Company, a department-store chain, many banks, vast amounts of real estate in and out of Utah (including 220,000 acres near Orlando, Florida), publishing companies, radio and television stations, and a big hunk of the *Los Angeles Times*. All this in exchange for the joys and burdens of polygamy—a remarkable deal, surely, though we recognize the judgment may not be unanimous.

Refusal

Thanks, but no thanks

Since 1898, membership in the National Institute of Arts and Letters has been one of the glittering prizes for American writers and other creative types. An invitation to join is considered the capstone of a career, and even such professional wild men as Allen Ginsberg and William Burroughs have been delighted to sign up. Consequently, the palm for second best refusal goes to Gore Vidal who, when he was invited to join, stated that he was declining the honor "because I already belong to the Diner's Club."

The best refusal? If historical significance is the criterion, it must be *il gran rifiuto*—"the great refusal," as Dante stigmatizes it in the *Inferno*.

This was the renunciation of his office by Pope Celestine V in 1294. Celestine was a cave-dwelling hermit before his elevation, and like Vidal today, a resident of Italy. As a result of his refusal, war broke out between the rival Colonna and Gaetani families; thousands were brutally slaughtered, and the city of Palestrina was razed and burned—a mise-en-scène even Vidal might envy.

Robot
(Personal)

"Klaatuu, barada nicto!"

Ever since Pygmalion persuaded the gods to animate Galatea, a statue of astonishing beauty, the idea of creating a simulacrum of man (or woman) has had a powerful grip on our imagination. It's a risky business, of course. Dr. Frankenstein's monster and the super-humanoids in Isaac Asimov's *I, Robot* spell it out for us: the closer we come to building a creature in our own image, the greater the peril. Yet most of the robots of contemporary fiction, like Robbie (*Forbidden Planet*), Klaatuu (*The Day the Earth Stood Still*), and the winsome R2-D2 (*Star Wars*), are wise and helpful servants—a sort of just reward for devising the technology that brought us the automatic teller and Mr. Coffee.

Unfortunately, given the current state of robotics, it'll be a long, long time before anybody builds a robot that could be considered even remotely acceptable as a fun date (unless your idea of a good time is being beaten at chess by something that looks as if it belonged on top of a squad car). The big money in robotics is concentrated in developing more, and more sophisticated, robot arms for the auto and steel industries.

However, there are a number of small and not-so-small companies that are spending an increasing amount of time, energy, and capital in developing robots for the individual consumer.

Admittedly, the robots currently available have rather limited applications. Walking the dog, taking out the garbage, or mowing the lawn stretches the capabilities of our state-of-the-art electronic friends to their limits. And although built-in computers mean several models are programmable, the problems in developing sensory technology are such that programs for even the simplest tasks must be tediously precise. Of course, most robots for the home *can* move around, and most can even claim an expandable memory.

We found sixteen manufacturers that produce robotics products, ranging from simple, two-wheeled, remote-controlled devices to sophisticated, independently mobile computers with ultrasonic and infrared sensory devices and fairly functional "arms."

At $4,500 (assembled) or $3,000 (unassembled)—and that price difference should tell you something—Heath Company's Hero 2000 is the best personal robot, featuring a built-in computer with 24K of RAM (expandable to 576K), a highly rated synthetic voice system, and an electronic arm.

Second best is also a Heath product. The Hero 1 is not as smart as the 2000, and its computer brain is expandable only to a modest 56K. But it does have just about every sensory device imaginable (both ultrasonic and infrared), a voice synthesizer, and an arm. Options available with Hero 1 include BASIC and courses in industrial electronics and robot applications—all enthusiastically described by Hero 1 in his own tinny version of the hard sell.

Unfortunately, the arm on both Heroes is relatively unsophisticated. Neither can carry loads of more than one pound; and while preparing a martini or a peanut-butter sandwich is not theoretically beyond their capabilities, such complex processes do presuppose that the mayonnaise and the Pernod are never where the Skippy's and the Boodles ought to be.

Second to second best is Arctec System's Gemini. Gemini has probably the most sophisticated sensory system currently available (nine ultrasonic sensors), as well as three separate microprocessors (one for the main control computer, one for the voice function, and one for motion control). What's more, when its batteries run down, the prudent little fellow will even look for a socket to recharge. Unfortunately, it does not (yet) come with an articulated arm, so at roughly $7,000 (assembled) or $3,595 (unassembled), we'll stick with Mr. Coffee.

Rock-and-Roll Album

Top of the pops

Iɴ 1979 Greil Marcus, the Berkeley-based rock critic, invited twenty of his peers, including Nick Tosces, Dave Marsh, Ellen Willis, Robert Cristgau, and Jay Cocks, to name the rock-and-roll record they'd take to a desert island. The result, *Stranded: Rock and Roll for a Desert Island*, contains some of the most engagingly quirky and personal rock criticism we know—including the late Lester Bangs' harrowing kudos to Van Morrison's *Astral Weeks*, which begins: "Van Morrison's *Astral Weeks* was released ten years ago, almost to the day, before this was written. It was particularly important to me because the fall of 1968 was such a terrible time: I was a physical and mental wreck, nerves shredded and ghosts and spiders looming and squatting across the mind."

The choices were eclectic, to say the least: the Rolling Stones' *Beggars Banquet*; *Presenting the Fabulous Ronettes Featuring Veronica* (arranged by Phil Spector); *The Wild, the Innocent, and the E Street Shuffle*, by you-know-who; *Trout Mask Replica,* by Captain Beefheart; the *Velvet Underground* (the compilation album, not to be confused with *The Velvet Underground*); *Desperado*, by the Eagles; *Something Else*, by the Kinks; *The Pretender*, by Jackson Browne; *The New York Dolls*; Huey "Piano" Smith's *Rock-and-Roll Revival!*; *Precious Lord: New Recordings of the Great Gospel Songs of Thomas A. Dorsey*; *Decade*, by Neil Young; *Living in the U.S.A.*, by Linda Ronstadt; *Dedicated to You*, by Ed Ward. Dave Marsh named a compilation album of his own devising called *Onan's Greatest Hits*, including Claudine Clark's "Party Lights" and the Stones' "Goin' Home." Desert islands, Marsh points out, can get to be lonely.

You will note some notable omissions here, e.g., anything by the Beatles, Dylan, or The Who. However, as Langdon Winner observes in his piece on Captain Beefheart, "Having lived in something of a shipwreck for the past several years, I understand that the question of which record I would want to play on a desert island must be taken literally. It is not a matter of what my favorite album happens to be. At issue is a kind of music rich enough, substantial enough to enable this castaway to endure a place of desolation over a very long haul." One thing you learn from collections like *Stranded* is that rock critics are desperate characters, engaged in a risky business, clinging to their review albums like drowning sailors to the wreck of the *Medusa*.

When Marcus asked for "the best," the Beatles *did* show up (not *Sgt. Pepper*, "which today seems artificial where *Rubber Soul* still seems full of life"); as did Bob Dylan and everyone else you might expect. The records most often mentioned were Dylan's *Highway 61 Revisited* and *Blonde on Blonde*; Chuck Berry's *Golden Decade* (and his *Greatest Hits*); *James Brown Alive at the Apollo*; *Rubber Soul*; Elvis's *Sun Sessions*; the

Stones' *Let It Bleed* and *Exile on Main Street*—"none of which anyone chose to write about"; and *Astral Weeks*.

People magazine's 1987 "Desert Island Top 10," inspired by the release of Bruce Springsteen's live albums, suggests there hasn't been a lot of activity in the Hall of Fame in this decade. Nobody they canvassed, for example, even mentioned *Live/1975–85*. *People*, having put the Boss on the cover for the umpteenth time, somewhat desperately rationalized this as "suggesting that even a hit of such critical magnitude must stand the test of time"—something which, presumably, Phil Collins' *No Jacket Required* (released a whole year before Springsteen's latest) or Paul Simon's *Graceland* (released a few weeks before) has done, since they do appear on the critics' top ten.

Time's Jay Cocks, who was consulted in both polls, forgot all about Huey "Piano" Smith, his earlier fave rave. Bob Dylan (*Biograph*) is now number one on his hit parade. Iggy Pop ecumenically named Miles Davis's *Sketches of Spain* and *Sinatra at the Sands*. Lynn Van Matre of the *Chicago Tribune* included Linton Kewsi Johnson's *Dread, Beat and Blood* (*that* sounds like fun), and Robbie Robertson filled out his scorecard with Krzysztof Penderecki's *Passio et Mors Domini Nostri Jesus Christi Secundum Lucam*, which never even entered the charts.

Yet another poll, this one conducted by British critic Paul Gambaccini, surveyed the choices of eighty-seven critics and pop-music figures in Great Britain and the United States. His final tally has fewer surprises. *Sgt. Pepper* tops the list (as it did in a Gambaccini survey ten years ago), followed in order by Springsteen's *Born to Run*; Dylan's *Blonde on Blonde*; Marvin Gaye's *What's Goin' On*; Springsteen's *Born in the U.S.A.*; Elvis's inevitable *Sun Sessions*; *The Velvet Underground and Nico* (not the compilation album included in Greil Marcus's desert-island survey—can't these rock critics make up their minds?); *Pet Sounds* by the Beach Boys; *Astral Weeks*; and *The Beatles*.

But *Los Angeles Times* music critic Robert Hilburn, who contributed to the poll, didn't agree with the outcome, and so, of course, we now have *his* top ten as well. Unexpectedly, it includes albums by artists other than Bruce Springsteen. His top pick is Elvis's *Sun Sessions* ("Holding up far better than debuts by the Beatles or the Stones, this album still reflects the innocence, celebrations and outlaw quality of rock and roll"). His runner-up is Dylan's *Highway 61 Revisited*; number three, *Plastic Ono Band*; number four, *Pepper*.

You begin to see the problem. In denominating the best, the critics conscientiously opt for albums which, for one reason or another, at one time or another, have changed rock, even if everyone is now sick to death of them and the kids like Bon Jovi better anyway. Keeping in mind the critical convention, and having consulted our own prejudices, then, the best rock-and-roll albums, in a tie, are *Sun Sessions*, *Astral Weeks*, *Rubber Soul*, *Blonde on Blonde*, and *Sgt. Pepper*. (*Pepper* hasn't aged as badly as some rock critics we could name.)

And second best? Right off, we knew it had to be a Stones album. This Struldbruggian over-the-hill gang hasn't been "The Greatest Rock-and-Roll Band in the World" since Altamont, but rockers they always were. True, the Dostoyevskian philosophical depths of "Sympathy for the Devil" have always eluded us, and "Gimme Shelter" from *Let It Bleed* ("the greatest rock-and-roll recording ever made," says Marcus) is still powerful, though it was always overblown. The records the Stones released as the sixties cultural revolution came to its edgy, equivocal conclusion have not worn well in our estimation.

We prefer *Aftermath*, *Between the Buttons*, and above all others the early compilation album *Big Hits (High Tide and Green Grass)*, which includes "Satisfaction," "It's All Over Now," and "Time Is on My Side"— work recorded when the sexual menace was believable and the Stones' strong misreading of the blues unadulterated by camp. Naming a "greatest hits" package as second best struck us for a while as a "cop-out" (to use a term current when the Stones were relevant). But *High Tide* is *not* available from K-Tel and it *was* produced in the first urgency of the

Stones' long, indeed apparently endless, career. And thus, on sober re-flection, it's second best.

Wait, there's more! (It's always too late to stop now with rock and roll, isn't it?) In the inventory "100 Best Albums of the Last Twenty Years," published in summer 1987 by *Rolling Stone*, there were few surprises in the top ten, which contained (counting from tenth to third places) *What's Goin' On*, by Marvin Gaye; the *White Album*; *Born to Run*; *Astral Weeks*; *The Rise and Fall of Ziggy Stardust and the Spiders from Mars*, by David Bowie; *Are You Experienced?* by the Jimi Hendrix Experience; *Plastic Ono Band*; and *Exile on Main Street*, the top Stones entry. Lodged improbably right below first-place *Sgt. Pepper* was the 1977 masterwork *Never Mind the Bollocks Here's the Sex Pistols*. Well, it's a thought.

Ronald Reagan Film

Where's the rest of him?

THE President's favorite, which he still shows in the White House, is *Kings Row* (Warner Brothers, 1942), directed by Sam Wood and co-starring Ann Sheridan and Robert Cummings. Jane Wyman once blamed the breakup of their marriage on his habit of screening this sturdy war-horse of the Late Late Show. "I just couldn't stand to watch *Kings Row* one more time," she explained.

As Tony Thomas points out in *The Films of Ronald Reagan*, the film's young leads were not the "obvious choices" to star in a film adapted from a Freudian period piece about incest, suicide, homosexuality, sexual repression, sadism, and mutilation in small-town America. Most of Reagan's earlier films had been light-weight B— movies on the order of *Girls on Probation*, *Tugboat Annie Sails Again*, and *Secret Service of the Air*, and his biggest fans were teenage girls. As biographer Garry Wills says, "He was the bobbysoxers' hero, the Tab Hunter of his day. . . . One of the studio's ways of cleaning up the novel was precisely to cast Reagan as the 'wicked' Drake McHugh. If he is as naughty as things get in town, then *Kings Row* cannot be so hellish after all."

Nonetheless, Reagan is genuinely affecting as the former playboy whose legs are needlessly amputated by a sadistic doctor (Charles Coburn). In his autobiography, he describes how he managed to work himself into a fugue state for the big scene when he discovers his missing legs and screams to Ann Sheridan, "Randy! Where's the rest of me?" Bob Cummings, from whom he stole the picture, has described *Kings Row* as the first "buddy" picture, and there is something to his interpretation. Andrew Sarris, film critic for the *Village Voice*, has written of the loverlike intensity with which Reagan, now that he is crippled, searches Cummings' face, when Cummings returns to Kings Row from his studies in Vienna with Doktor Freud.

Apart from estimable work by the Warner Brothers repertory company, notably Maria Ouspenskaya, *Kings Row* is remarkable for its arty, semi-expressionist photography and sets. James Wong Howe was the cinematographer, and the production designer was the legendary William Cameron Menzies.

Contrary to myth, Reagan made his share of "A" features before his star fell and politics, the "G.E. Theater," and a brief stint in Vegas distracted him. He was generally cast as a nice guy ("No, no," Jack L. Warner is supposed to have cried, "Jimmy Stewart for governor! Ronald Reagan for best friend!"), but otherwise, his roles were impressively varied. He was an idealistic young attorney (*Girls on Probation*), a college professor (*Bedtime for Bonzo* and again in *She's Working Her Way Through College*), a gay playboy (*Dark Victory*), a veterinarian (*Stallion Road*), a drifter (*Juke Girl*), an army sergeant (*The Voice of the Turtle*), a gangster (*The Killers*, his last picture, in which he belts Angie Dickinson), a Broadway producer (*An Angel from Texas*), a hard-bitten mercenary (*Hong Kong*), and an epileptic biochemist (*Night unto Night*, with Viveca Lindfors). Not to mention Knute Rockne; Grover Cleveland Alexander, the alcoholic baseball great; and George Armstrong Custer. In his best comedy, *The Girl from Jones Beach*, Reagan insinuates himself into an art class taught by Virginia Mayo by posing as a recent arrival from Czechoslovakia.

Ironically, as Wills points out, Reagan's undoing as an actor was that he was too ambitious. The studios had slotted him as a light romantic lead with a flair for comedy, on the order of Van Johnson, Peter Lawford, and Gig Young—"not a bad league," as Wills says, but he longed for action and cowboy roles. "Reagan failed in Hollywood because he was not satisfied with his proper rung, with the range he commanded, but attempted heavier roles he could not sustain. These spiraled him downward from *The Last Outpost* (1951) to *Hellcats of the Navy* (1955), and even to *The Killers* (1964)."

The Hasty Heart (1950), Ronald Reagan's second best film, was his last major commercial success on the big screen. It must have been a nightmare to shoot. Set in a British military hospital in steamy tropical Burma, the picture was filmed in England, during one of the coldest winters of the century. (The Labor government had limited the amount of currency that could be taken out of the country, so the studios were filming there to use up profits that would otherwise have been frozen.) His divorce from Jane Wyman had just become final, and even the steaks in boxes he had sent from "21" in New York to his suite at the Savoy Hotel were regularly stolen. (Meat was still being rationed in England.)

Reagan plays "Yank," a happy warrior who attempts to befriend Lachie (Richard Todd), a closemouthed, standoffish young Scot who (as the others learn) is dying. When Todd spurns what he thinks is the others' pity, Reagan blows up, telling him that in his pride he will die alone—

"sorrow is born in the hasty heart." It's a genuinely moving scene (Reagan, incidentally, had hoped to play the younger man's part himself), and the reviews were excellent.

Director Vincent Sherman remembers that the fog was so heavy that winter that the limousine carrying Reagan and his costars would sometimes take two or three hours to travel from the Savoy to the Elstree studio. "My experience in directing him was most pleasant. He was easy to work with, always knew his lines, was conscientious and took direction. . . . I wish I could give a more colorful account, but Ronnie was a well-behaved, easygoing professional actor who was never involved in any serious scandal or Hollywood peccadillo. This does not make for an exciting personality. . . ."

In 1952 Reagan left Warners'. A decade later, *The Killers*, his last movie, had a theatrical release only because it was considered too violent for television. He is said to have planned a comeback as a character actor specializing in villains, but it didn't work—and the rest is history.

Running Shoes

Fleet feet

REMEMBER sneakers? No? There used to be just two kinds: those for guys and those for girls. Now we have motion-control shoes, cushioned shoes, high-mileage shoes. Shoes for pronators, supinators, forefoot strikers, midfoot strikers, and cross-country runners (not to mention shoes for pronators who are also forefoot-striking cross-country runners).

We asked a friend who runs a sports-injury prevention center to be our informant in these matters. "Pronators lean forward, supinators lean back," he informed us. "The way your foot strikes the ground determines how your body absorbs the force of the impact. Running shoes are designed to compensate for variations in running styles. People who land on their forefoot, for example, need a shoe with extra cushioning there.

"Most people who run for exercise don't know how to buy shoes. They buy for looks or because they feel comfortable when they try them on in the store. A good way to find out what kind of shoe you need is to run for a while in a good pair of basic running shoes and see how they wear." If your shoes tend to get pushed over sideways, you're probably rolling to one side each time your foot strikes the ground. If you're leaning forward or leaning back, a new pair of running shoes will exaggerate that motion slightly.

Motion-control shoes have a wide sole designed to compensate for runners who tend to land on the sides of their feet or who are severe pronators or supinators. Nike Venue, Puma Tahara, Kangaroos Coil R1, Adidas Silverstar, Reebok GL6000, Converse Revenge and the Brooks Nexus all have wide, side-cushioned soles and have been highly rated by runners, but because of the design variations, you need to experiment to see which is your personal best.

For forefoot strikers, or anyone who runs long distances on hard, unforgiving surfaces, there are the cushioned shoes. Reebok DL5600, New Balance 735, Brooks Response, and Nike Pegasus Plus all get high marks in this category. Turntec's Quixote Plus also ranks right up there with the best of the cushioned shoes, but is generally priced much lower.

Runners who need both motion-control compensation and extra cushioning should try one of these all-around shoes: Kangaroos Omnicoil, Nike Venue, Avia600, Turntec Quixote Plus (and Lady Quixote Plus), Tiger GTII, Brooks Trilogy, and Saucony's Shadow and Lady Shadow.

If you are male and weigh more than 180 pounds, you need a shoe that softens those heavy blows. Kangaroos Coil R1 and R2, Brooks Chariot KW, Puma RS100, Etonic Aura, and Tiger Striker ST (best value in this category) are all tough contenders designed to withstand heavy shock and bear up under the stress of the greater torque of larger runners. For big women, the Etonic Lady Sigma, New Balance W520 and Brooks Chariot are excellent choices.

For cross-country runners, particularly those who enjoy the unpaved delights of a sylvan environment, the Hersey High Top custom design may be your shoe, if you can afford it. Hersey designs each pair specifically for you.

For those with a deeply ingrained competitive urge who like to run fast if not far, there are specially built racing shoes. At the top of this category is the neon yellow, neon orange, blue, and white Nike Tiger Freak, designed, we suspect, to appeal as much to the ego of the racer as to provide for his or her specific physical requirements. Only for runners with excellent form or those who just like to *look* fast when they're standing still.

Now for the second best. This is still a permissive society (at least where foot fashion is concerned), and many of us like to wear our running shoes all day long. When we walk into a room, we don't want to draw undue attention to our feet (as we would with a pair of Tiger Freaks). And most of us don't need special features designed to correct our running style. We want comfort, support, style, and—let's face it—economy.

This is the realm of the basic running shoe. The Nike Windrunner, Converse Gazelle, Puma Deity, Brooks Response, Turntec Quixote Plus, Etonic Trans-Am Trainer, and Kangaroos Aussie II are all highly rated for low-mileage runners with no biomechanical problems. Our choice for second best is Reebok's LC1500 for men and the LC3000 for women.

San Francisco Coffeehouse

*"O Paradiso! sings
the jukebox"*

WHERE, we ask you, has the coffeehouse flourished with so much panache, sheltered so many scribblers, or spawned so many legends as in San Francisco? Yes, the coffeehouse had a good run in Boswell's London, not to mention Wittgenstein's Vienna, but hey! the past is prologue. The North Beach San Francisco coffeehouse scene is a living legend.

Of course it's the mise-en-scène that counts—the gleaming espresso machines, the marble-topped tables, the cavernous, memoried rooms, the opportunity to wear a black turtleneck sweater and look Byronic. Not to mention those *mysterioso* foggy nights. (Mostly occurring in July or

August: "The coldest winter I ever spent was summer in San Francisco"—
Mark Twain.)

Whiling away an afternoon with a notebook and a tamarindo is perfectly permissible. But it helps that the cappuccinos in North Beach are strong enough to strip the chrome from the exhaust pipe of a '57 Chevy. If coffee consumption is declining among health-conscious Baby Boomers, San Franciso hasn't heard about it. Throughout the Bay Area, passionate debate rages over the respective merits of java ground by Grafeo and by Peet's.

Squeezed between Chinatown and the Financial District, North Beach still breathes the last enchantments of the 1950s. Where Kerouac and Ginsberg scribbled, we can dawdle. The ancient Italian roots of this part of the City are withering (but there's still the whiff of codfish around the old markets); and the Carol Doda era of topless-bottomless entertainment is dying out in the blue-nosed, Ed Meese 1980s. But the coffeehouses survive.

Frankly, our favorite North Beach perch is Vesuvio at 255 Columbus, next door to City Lights, the famously hip bookstore presided over by poet Lawrence Ferlinghetti. Founded by the legendary San Francisco character Henri Lenoir, frequented (notably on his last, fatal American tour) by Dylan Thomas, Vesuvio (*not* Vesuvio's) is our idea of a place to drink. Which, perhaps, should disqualify it from this category. Vesuvio, after all, is a bar more than coffeehouse.

Tosca, on Columbus across from City Lights, has a lovely jukebox (heavy on opera), and the distinction of having 86'd Bob Dylan. (Allen Ginsberg, who witnessed this enormity, has never gone back.) Sam Shepard hangs out here when in San Francisco, and brought the stars and crew of *The Right Stuff* with him, when Phil Kaufman was shooting the film.

But Caffe Trieste! Only a knight's move away, you can still see Allen Ginsberg on his visits to the City. This is a coffeehouse. Brooding over your espresso romano, you can plunk your cup on the very coffee ring

Jack Kerouac left while speedwriting *On the Road*. It's high-ceilinged, blue with the smoke from French cigarettes, surprisingly small, and utterly unchanged. As San Francisco poet Harold Norse wrote (we're quoting Don Herron's invaluable *The Literary World of San Francisco* quoting Norse):

> *here in San Francisco*
> *as I sit at the Trieste*
> *—recitative of years!*
> *O Paradiso! sings the jukebox*
> *as Virgil and Verdi combine*
> *in this life*
> *to produce the only Golden Age*
> *there'll be.*

According to Herron, Francis Ford Coppola finished the screenplay of *The Godfather* at the Trieste. Whether all of this amounts to a golden age, we can't say, but this lovable anachronism is definitely second best by us.

Scenic
Drive

A Swiss no miss

NOT those dramatic curves and cliffs on Route 1 along the Pacific from ruggedly green Big Sur across the Golden Gate and on to Bodega Bay (the sun gets in your eyes). Not Miami to Key West (boring even in a blue or green or bird-of-paradise sunset after the first fifteen minutes). Not Route 66 (the Burma Shave signs are all gone). Not the Corniche (lunch is too expensive).

Maybe Città di Castello to Bomarzo along the Tiber in Umbria (between Florence and Rome). There are twisty, rugged mountain roads to challenge your Ferrari. Magnificent Renaissance cities, built on medieval and Etruscan foundations, are untouched by the imagination of a

Gropius. And there's some weird stuff too: in the valley north of Bom-arzo, gigantic tufa rocks, bigger than houses, have been carved by an unknown artist into mythic, hallucinogenic shapes—half men, half monsters; a giant ripping limbs from an unfortunate opponent; triple-headed Cerberus; and a stone tortoise as big as a Volkswagen bus. In the Duomo at Orvieto, murals begun by Fra Angelico conclude with a Bosch-like series by Signorelli that vividly depicts Dante's Apocalypse. And the hotels are cheap.

Or maybe Heidelberg to Munich, on Germany's Romantische Strasse. From the storybook castles of the Neckar, through the Black Forest to Lake Constance and into the Alps, this drive through history includes a pass by Mad Ludwig's Neuschwanstein, a must-see, despite its dubious status as the most photographed castle in the world. Walt Disney de-signed *his* castle after it, but he shied away from copying the interior, which includes an artificial cavern, leading from the bedroom to the kitchen, to satisfy the odd urge for royal snack, and a canopy above the royal bed that depicts, in meticulously carved wood, the spires of all the German cathedrals. The effect is not one of religious exaltation.

Those are excellent drives, but our choice for second best is even more magnificent. The only reason it can't legitimately be included among the best is that, even though you make the whole journey by car, there isn't much driving to do.

You must try it in the daytime, in winter, on a clear day. In the Swiss village of Kandersteg you drive through the train station and onto a train. Thoughtful attendants lash your Porsche to the flatbed. As you cross the roof of the world, open your Swiss Spatlese and pull out the Appenzeller Kase you thoughtfully provided yourself with back in Spiez or Thun and finish it off with a little schnapps before a refreshing nap and the descent into the Rhône Valley. We recommend you take a friend.

Single-Malt Scotch

THE Irish might have invented it, but it was the Scots who *perfected* the manufacture of whiskey, despite what you might hear in Canada, Kentucky, or Dublin. Single-malt, or "glen," scotch is still distilled by the same methods as it was seven centuries ago when the soldiers of King Henry II first encountered *usquebaugh* (water of life) during an invasion of the Emerald Isles. Its only ingredients, then and now, are sprouted (malted) barley and the pure waters of Scottish springs and brooks.

The malt is dried above smoldering peat which imparts that distinctive smoky tang to the final product. Local waters are added to the malt and the resulting "wort" allowed to ferment. This mixture then goes into the first of a series of pot stills for distillation. (The copper pots used for the distillation process are believed to be possessed of magical properties, and distillers take great care to placate the spirits of the stills. When parts of the pots wear out and must be replaced, the dents and nicks on the old parts are faithfully reproduced on the new. Distillers aren't sure if this does any good, but none dare alter the tradition.) The final distillation is put into well-used oak casks for mellowing.

Until recently, single-malts were virtually a secret Scots kept to themselves (and many drinkers accustomed to blended whiskies still think it's a secret they can keep). But they're growing in favor among sophisticated imbibers here and in Asia, and the finer varieties, taken neat, are a superb alternative to cognac or Armagnac as an after-dinner drink. There are about twenty different brands available in retail shops. The strong, distinctive taste may not be everyone's favorite tipple, but those with a palate for scotch will definitely find an exploration into single-malts rewarding.

The Glenlivet (the definite article is part of the name) is most frequently regarded as the glen scotch to compare all others by, and certainly the Glenlivet has tradition on its side, coming as it does from the oldest (1823) legally licensed distillery in Scotland. This single-malt is smooth, slightly sweet, and in deference to conventional wisdom, would have to be nominated as the best. But here again, second best is probably the connoisseur's preference.

Laphroaig, 90.4 proof, aged ten years, and hailing from Islay, home of the "fullest" or "biggest" glen whiskeys, is formidable indeed. It's smoky as a forest fire, has a fine salt-tang, and is dense with peat. The uninitiated often compare Laphroaig's taste to iodine, finding it "medicinal," but in blind taste tests it scores first with impressive frequency—even in California, where the standard tipple is Calistoga water, and a glass of white wine is considered a binge.

Ski
School

Buy the book

SANKT ANTON, Austria, is the home of the finest ski school in the world. Government certified instructors, fluent in three or more languages, teach classes ranging from beginner through expert with such kindness, tact, and zest that you may find yourself hurtling effortlessly down the *piste* faster than you can say "Anschluss." And upon graduation you receive a spiffy wallet-sized certificate with your photo on it, filled with official-looking stamps and signatures.

Unfortunately, Sankt Anton is rather inconveniently located on another continent, so we must make do with what we can find on the slopes of our own resorts. Most profit-minded American lift-operators are unwilling to invest heavily in their ski schools, so finding a good instructor is mostly a function of luck. There are a few exceptions, notably at Stowe, Vermont; Vail, Colorado; and Squaw Valley, California. But even at those resorts, the best instruction is reserved for beginners (to fuel the expanding market), and anyone with more than a few weeks' experience has to try to figure out alone how to break through to an advanced technique.

For a while there was a ski workshop at Squaw Valley designed to make advanced skiers out of intermediates in just one week. The workshop was run by writer-instructor Lito Tejada-Flores (we don't make these names up) and was so wildly successful that it is now legendary in western skiing circles. Unfortunately, however, it closed several years ago. But we are indebted to the Squaw workshop for producing the second best ski school, which you can attend wherever you can find snow and a downhill slope.

The success Mr. Tejada-Flores experienced at Squaw encouraged him to develop a self-programmed teaching guide for intermediate skiers (although he also includes a detailed chapter for beginners). And the amazing thing is, it works. *Breakthrough on Skis: How to Get Out of the Intermediate Rut* clearly explains the techniques required to master the art of dancing with apparently effortless ease down even the most challenging slopes. A week on the slopes with Mr. Tejada-Flores' book is almost guaranteed to produce remarkable results. And at $8.95, it's a lot cheaper than lessons.

A book is no substitute for the hands-on instruction beginners need to become oriented to skis and slopes, but for anyone who can do a stem christie (beginner to intermediate level), this guide will provide a clearer explication of the techniques of advanced skiing, and offers more efficient exercises, than you are likely to find with all but a very few of the best instructors. And Mr. Tejada-Flores is a gifted writer whose love of skiing and mountain landscapes enlivens what might otherwise be dull technical reading.

Skyscraper Design

"Tall, every inch of it tall"

LIKE Yankee Doodle, jazz, Big Macs, and the blues, the modern skyscraper was born in the U.S.A. Its cradles were Chicago and New York City at the turn of the century, and its most gifted designers have been native or born-again Americans like Louis Sullivan, Raymond Hood, Frank Lloyd Wright, Philip Johnson, Mies van der Rohe, and I. M. Pei. Its grandest examples are to be found looming like massive paleoliths over the Lake Shore and the streets of Manhattan.

The history of the skyscraper registers, first of all, what Paul Goldberger of the *New York Times* calls the long "aesthetic duel" between Chicago and New York. In Chicago, there are the severe Monadnock and Reliance towers; in New York, the splendiferous Woolworth Building. Yet by the twenties, the two aesthetics were synthesized in the art deco splendor of the Chrysler Building—as characteristic a product of the Jazz Age as *The Great Gatsby*.

The thirties brought the solid monumentalism of the Empire State Building and Rockefeller Center, followed, after the war, by the triumph of the international style and its "glass boxes." Now, of course, we live in the strange new era of "postmodern" skyscrapers, most notoriously symbolized by Philip Johnson's AT & T headquarters, a thirty-four-story Chippendale highboy.

Probably no architectural critic would point to the Empire State Building as the most stylish skyscraper ever designed, which will not deter *us* from naming it the best. If a skyscraper "must be tall, every inch of it tall . . . rising in sheer exaltation from top to bottom without a single dissenting line," as Louis Sullivan said, then the Empire State Building is the paradigmatic skyscraper. Critic Goldberger writes, "The Empire State, even more than the Chrysler Building, became a symbol not only of the New York skyline, but of tall buildings everywhere . . . a natural wonder as much as a building, a phenomenon that would enter the popular lore." For decades, of course, the Empire State was the tallest man-made structure on the planet, and frankly, when it ceased to be, we stopped counting.

Second best? Louis Sullivan is virtually synonymous with the development of the skyscraper. Yet many of his greatest designs, like the ten-story brick-and-terra-cotta Wainwright Building in St. Louis (1891), are scarcely even high rises in the contemporary sense. Our dictionary defines *skyscraper*, architecturally speaking, as "a building completely supported by a framework of girders, as opposed to one supported by load-bearing walls." The startlingly contemporary, proto-brutalist Monadnock Building (Burnham and Root, 1891) is a walled structure, but has so much prophetic force we're tempted to nominate *it*, and stop searching.

Daniel H. Burnham's wedge-shaped, much photographed Flatiron

Building in New York (1903), Hood and Howells' gothic Chicago Trib-une Tower, Goodhue's Nebraska State Capitol, the American Radiator Building, the General Electric Building, the Chrysler Building (of course), the Seagram Building—we could go on—all have merit or historical influence or both to recommend them.

It's tempting, again, to pay homage to a particular genius of the skyscraper form, like Raymond Hood or Philip Johnson—Johnson has a positively Stravinskyan capacity for shedding and adopting new styles. Among Johnson and Burgee designs, we have been particularly dazzled in recent decades by the "humanistic" IDS Center in Minneapolis; the "abstract" Pennzoil Plaza in Houston (trapezoidal towers, sliced at forty-five-degree angles at the top); and the stepped-back towers of the Re-public Bank Building, also in Houston.

Another tempting possibility is to name a great *unbuilt* design. The competition to design a new headquarters for the *Chicago Tribune* in 1922 ($50,000 for the winning entry) was "one of the great architectural events of the early part of the century." Walter Gropius and Adolf Loos were among the entrants, but few *built* buildings have had the influence of Eliel Saarinen's losing stepped-back design, which, among other things, became a lodestar for the winner, Raymond Hood.

But finally, for second best, we're going for the Woolworth Building in Manhattan (1913), designed by Cass Gilbert. "Zealously Gothic in its details, down to terra-cotta gargoyles and buttresses," twenty-nine stories high in a U-shape, it was a true wonder of the world when it was built—the tallest building in the world, in fact, housing fourteen thou-sand workers who could speed to the top in twenty-nine elevators, in-cluding two operating express from ground floor to the fifty-fourth-story aerie.

"The mix of delicacy and strength has an almost Mozartian quality to it," says Goldberger, describing what is still Woolworth's headquarters, "a sense of light, graceful detail applied to a firm and self-assured struc-ture. One of the most remarkable skyscrapers ever built."

Sports Event

The Super Duper Bowl

NOWHERE is the pressure to be number one, to avoid being second best, more pronounced than in sports. Grantland Rice's poetic dictum "It matters not if you win or lose, but how you play the game" has long since been replaced by Leo Durocher's "Nice guys finish last" and Vince Lombardi's "Winning isn't everything, it's the *only* thing." Gentle urgings toward sportsmanship are replaced on coaches' lips by "Show me a good loser and I'll show you a loser."

In the competition for the number one sports event, every American knows who the winner is: Pete Rozelle and the National Football League with its super-successful Super Bowl.

It has the largest annual audience of anything on television, sports or nonsports. And those 130 million or so viewers bring in the highest advertising revenue on television, more than half a million dollars per thirty-second spot. In less than a quarter century, this media spectacle has surpassed such Goliaths of spectator sports as the World Series, the NCAA and NBA play-offs, the Derbies from Kentucky to Soap Box to Roller, the NHL final face-offs, and the Kewanee, Illinois, Hog Days.

But, surprise of surprises to the Yankee public, the Super Bowl is a distant second in world competition, lagging far behind the world's number one sports event, the World Cup soccer play-offs. American life may come to a standstill on Super Sunday in January, with warnings to viewers not to flush their toilets all at the same time during time-outs lest urban water systems be destroyed. But once every four years an insane frenzy spreads across several hundred other nations around the globe *at the same time*, as their national teams struggle toward the world's number one impossible dream, the World Cup. As many as two billion watch this competition on television, dwarfing the comparatively less-than-super Super Bowl audience.

The world's number one sport also has the distinction of unleashing the famous "Soccer War," when Honduras and El Salvador decided to settle with troops what their *futbol* players couldn't. But that war proved less bloody than the 1985 charge by Liverpool fans against Italian fans in which forty people died, or the death of sixty-six soccer fans in Glasgow in 1966, or the 264 fatalities after an Argentina-Peru soccer game in 1964. These are fans who care!

But the grace and fire of soccer has failed to capture the imagination of the American public—or at least the interest of television programmers, who recognize a sport that lacks convenient TV time-outs when they see one.

But where the number one sport has continuous action, the second best has *impact*. In American football, a hit is a hit is a hit. Watching it is far preferable to playing it. Let's face it, who in their right mind—or for less than $80,000—wants to run down a long field full tilt under a kick while agile, well-muscled 260-pound behemoths take aim at your one and only body? Who wants to run a crossing pattern while defensive backs get a gleam in their eye like Jack Nicklaus eyeing a well-teed golf ball? It's no coincidence that the second best sport is a *spectator* sport.

How appropriate that America's number one sports event happens on what was once the Sabbath, the holy day. In the annual liturgical cycle of modern America, the two-game Sunday gradually builds to a climax as it spills over into Monday night and even Saturdays until, just before the Big One, it enters into a final two weeks of purifying penance when *nothing happens*! Two weeks of *coitus interruptus*, cold turkey, while sports journalists frantically interview players' relatives down to three generations removed, and speculation mounts as to why the stock market gets bullish only when the NFC wins (or is it the AFC?).

Like Advent and Lent, this penance works. By Super Sunday, since nothing has happened for two weeks, the entire American public forgets the actual game experience of two decades or more and comes to expect that on *this* Super Sunday, the game will be close. Well, maybe not close, but at least there will be decisive plays. Or, if not that, maybe somebody will get destroyed, or maybe a coach will scratch his crotch in front of 130 million viewers, or maybe a new Macintosh commercial will air, or maybe the Goodyear blimp will explode like in *Black Sunday* and eliminate the entirety of America's corporate elite along with a few of its oversized athletes.

Watching, and partying for, the Super Bowl have become *de rigueur*. In fact, to be labeled a dangerous rebel, one can outdo Camus or Kropotkin simply by asking, "What Super Bowl?" Howard Cosell has out-talked Moses; Vince Lombardi moved aside the Buddha with an inside trap block; Atlas is an interior lineman; Mercury catches passes and returns punts; Adonis calls plays and throws the ball. Even Aphrodite and Hera have a place, but only as supporting cast waving pom-poms and serving finger food.

Each January it comes around, giving a fixity and purpose to our national calendar. And each January we tune in, turn on, and drop out of normal consciousness to slide into the larger-than-life world of epic sagas and Promethean struggles—sagas of too few tickets and too many commercials, struggles to keep attentive amid programmed emotions and scheduled highs.

But dare we speak irreverently of America's number one sports event, and dare we call it second best? Of course, in these pages we can. For what true super fan would ever look at a book called, heresy of heresies, *The (Second) Best?*

Tap
Water

Spouting off

Not the water of Niagara Falls, which passes through several toxic-waste dump sites, including Love Canal's, before it reaches the taps of that city. Not New Orleans, which draws its drinking water from the Mississippi at a point where it contains so much organic waste that it has been described in the *New York Times* as "the colon of America." Certainly not the saline solution that comes out of San Diego faucets—thinking about the number of kidneys and irrigated fields the water of *that* city has passed through would give pause even to the thirsty.

The best is from New York City, which draws its water from a series of reservoirs in the Catskills. Whether by accident or design, the architects of its waterworks sixty years ago selected an area so fortunately situated that it remains free of the acid rainfall that pollutes water farther to the north. New Yorkers, proud of their water, bottle it and take it along on trips to less privileged parts of the country, which is to say everywhere else. Unfortunately, all that wonderful H_2O must pass through a rotting pipe system, so quality within the city tends to vary widely.

For second best we nominate the water of Seattle. It is even softer and purer than New York City water, but lacks that tonic, mineral, Manhattan tang. Drink it straight from the tap and it tastes of the pure Cascade Mountain springs from whence it comes. The tiny touch of chlorine with which Seattle's water is treated is detectable only after the water has been exposed to the air for a few minutes. So drink it fast!

Taxicab
Service

Not just taken for a ride

THE English Channel island of Sark has the best taxi service in the world. Motor vehicles are forbidden on Sark, so the taxis are actually horse-drawn carriages. This poses no great hardship to the visitor, as there isn't really anyplace to go. Sark is only three and a half miles long. But sitting behind a clopping horse in a plush antique carriage, you can ride up and across the narrow spine of an isthmus that rises 250 feet above the sea and connects Sark with Little Sark, while your driver regales you with tales from the island's rich history (it may very well have been Sark that the Spanish Armada ran into on its way to England). Then, because there is nothing to do in Little Sark either, you can ride back to Sark, where there is a pub.

London has the second best taxi service. Not only are the cabs clean and comfortable, but the drivers are all graduates of a special school. Competition to get in is tough, and graduation requirements are incredible. Candidates for cabbiehood must recite entire routes between given destinations (which may only be the names of pubs), taking one-way streets and temporary closures into account. And if the route they give the examiners (orally) contains a single mistake, or if it's not the shortest route, they fail! They must also demonstrate a thorough understanding of London's history, and they are expected to be prepared to give reliable advice on restaurants and entertainment. The understandably proud graduates refer to this arduous training as "Getting the Knowledge." New Yorkers, normally shockproof, frequently overtip.

Think Tank

Tops in the mind field

THE late Herman Kahn was a jolly fat man whose occupation was thinking about the unthinkable—first for the RAND Corporation, where his specialty was thermonuclear war, and later at his own Hudson Institute. The story is told that one day Kahn held up a single piece of paper, waved it in a visitor's face, giggled, and said: "See this? It's worth three million dollars."

Think tanks represent the most prestigious and shadowy wing of the immense research-and-development empire that sprang up in the U.S. during and after World War II. It's not strictly true to say they produce nothing but words; writing in 1971, Paul Dickson in his book *Think Tanks* listed among the products hatched by systematic R & D a vaccine for German measles, the space program, freeze-dried coffee, solid-state electronics, xerography, the H-bomb, and the modern computer.

Today, there are upwards of a thousand U.S. institutes and firms in the research-and-development empire that qualify as true "think tanks"— i.e., permanent, autonomous institutions "devoted to modern policy-making and the brokerage of technology." Some are attached to universities, like the Stanford Research Institute (SRI), and several score are attached to the federal government, for which they ponder everything from cancer research to waging nuclear war. The most famous of these is "Mother RAND," based in Santa Monica, California.

Then there are also several hundred private firms that think for a fee. "They are reminiscent of the *condottieri* bands of medieval Italy who offered skilled soldiers to the highest bidder," says Dickson. They will design a cigarette filter, devise an investment strategy, reorganize your corporation's management hierarchy, or rethink its identity. But this business is by no means new; the venerable firm of Arthur D. Little, Inc., was functioning as a think tank long before the term (which goes back to the forties) was coined.

Finally, there is an elite handful of independent, public policy institutes whose support comes from like-minded foundations. (Some also solicit federal money for particular projects.) Their paper products include journals; symposia proceedings; books; and, lately, television and radio programs. Their fellows include such national figures as economist Milton Friedman (at Hoover Institute) and Jeane Kirkpatrick (at Georgetown's Center for Strategic and International Studies).

Paradoxically, except for Ralph Nader's Center for the Study of Responsive Law ("Nader's Raiders"), the public policy think tanks are mostly unknown to the average citizen whose life they affect every day. "Our targets are the policy-makers and the opinion-making elite," says Burton Y. Pines of the conservative Heritage Institute. "The public gets it from them."

Most of the policy institutes are located in Washington, D.C., and are staffed with phalanxes of youngish Ph.D.'s. However, there's also a concentration in California, and some mavericks—even a few dropouts—can be found in their cloisters. Ronald Reagan's "favorite" think tank is said to be the Institute for Contemporary Studies, a quirky "New Age" outfit in San Francisco. The most influential include the Brookings Institute, the American Enterprise Institute (AEI), the left-of-center Institute for Policy Studies, and the right-of-center Heritage Institute, all located within the D.C. beltway. The conservative Hoover Institute is on the Stanford campus in Palo Alto, California. Ronald Reagan and Alexander Solzhenitsyn are Honorary Fellows.

Leaving aside the technoids and the Strangelovian netherworld of the "defense intellectuals," who are the best and second best among this group? After all, it's our hearts and minds they're after.

Tops for service, solidity, and continuing influence is the elderly Brookings Institute, which has existed in its present form since 1927, operating from a stately home on Massachusetts Avenue. Its studies range from financial arcana to broad-gauge policy formulation. In the thirties it harried FDR's New Deal, but by Harry Truman's time it was fine-tuning the Marshall Plan that resurrected postwar Europe. One of its traditions is presenting every incoming president with a report on the state of the union. Relations with the White House were particularly close under JFK and LBJ, who told Brookings, "You are a national institution . . . if you did not exist we would have to ask someone to invent you." Relations with Richard Nixon's administration were less cordial. His counsel, Charles Colson, allegedly proposed firebombing Brookings—or at least setting up a conservative counterpart, to be run by the distinguished novelist and plumber E. Howard Hunt.

Actually, its conservative counterpart, the American Enterprise Institute, had been around since 1943. Today, AEI's public profile is higher than Brookings', and its influence on the Reagan administration has been immense. If we rank it second best, this is because it grew up in

Brookings' shadow, and the older institute is still its model—not because it's second in intellectual liveliness or influence. This is the institute that virtually staffed Ronald Reagan's White House in his first term.

AEI was founded in 1943 by Lewis H. Brown, an anti-New Deal corporation executive (president of the Johns-Manville Corporation). As Sidney Blumenthal of the *Washington Post* notes in his *The Rise of the Counter-Establishment,* "It has a budget of $80,000, no resident scholars, and no reputation. . . . In Washington, it was less well known than most corner drugstores," and it continued to be obscure right up to Brown's death in 1953. Today, there are over three hundred staffers and adjunct scholars; it publishes four magazines (*Regulation, Public Opinion, The AEI Economist, Foreign Policy and Defense Review*), and produces a monthly television show and weekly radio programs. Since the mid-fifties AEI has been run in succession by the William Baroodys, *père et fils,* a formidable pair of policy brokers and publicists. Baroody senior made AEI a bastion of free-market economics and spearheaded Barry Goldwater's presidential candidacy in 1964. Under Baroody junior, AEI's alliance with corporate America was cemented, and its rise to national prominence completed. Today, even David Rockefeller has nothing but nice things to say about it.

One of AEI's biggest causes has been deregulation (you might remember that, the next time you read about yet another near miss over J.F.K. or O'Hare). Oddly enough, for many years this conservative bulwark cast a cold eye on Ronald Reagan. Baroody senior wasn't sure he wanted a Hollywood actor associated with Barry Goldwater, and in 1980 the institute's favorite was George Bush. But this hasn't kept AEI from being, as one of its fellows put it, "the flagship of conservatism"—and number two brains trust in the country.

Thirst Quencher

A tall glass of bubbly club

Club soda. Best is uncarbonated water (Evian or tap, as you prefer). Following club soda, in order, are iced tea, diet cola, pre-sweetened Kool-Aid, beer, ginger ale, and milk.

35-mm Camera

Candid computer

COMPACT, elegant, lightweight, crammed with microchip-driven versatility, the 35-mm camera is now a requisite component of the arsenals of both amateur and professional photographers. But it wasn't always so. Professionals were slow to see the advantages back in 1932 when Leica and Zeiss Contax first appeared on the American market. But despite the drawback of a relatively small (and therefore grainy) negative, there were a few adventurers who saw opportunity in the handy new small-format camera.

Margaret Bourke-White used a Leica to cover the trial of Bruno Hauptman in 1935, and a year later Alfred Stieglitz caught Ansel Adams toying with a Zeiss Contax. "If I were younger and had one of those little cameras," said the old master, "I'd lock the place up for half the time and go out into the streets and catch the life of the city." Although Adams is best known for his work with larger formats, his portraiture, such as the famous shot of Georgia O'Keeffe and Orville Cox, demonstrates his later mastery of 35-mm as well.

While Leica and Contax still have a reputation to be reckoned with, it is the Japanese manufacturers who, in an awesome frenzy of competition, have been setting the trend for the past few decades. In 1978 Canon introduced the A1, the first (and still one of the finest) automatic 35-mm single-lens reflex (SLR) camera. Capable of automatically setting either the aperture or the shutter speed (or both in the programmed automation mode), it was the user-friendliest 35-mm ever made. In a single stroke the market was expanded to include everyone who couldn't read an in-camera exposure meter (or didn't care to) and turn a knob.

Other manufacturers brought out their own versions of programmable machines, but a final refinement was needed to further free the new generation of 35-mm SLRs from the biological fallibility of the photographer's eye. To build a camera that would focus itself, a system had to be designed that could tell the camera exactly how to set the lenses for a sharp focus, even within the narrow depths of field dictated by low-speed film or low-light conditions.

The solution is an ingenious combination of light-sensitive silicon chips with the latest in miniature-machine technology. In most systems, as many as three narrowly focused microchip couple control devices (CCDs) measure the degree of contrast at the center of the image. The highest possible average contrast means there are the fewest gray areas in the image, resulting in a sharp focus. "Only the human eye focuses faster," says the ad for the Minolta Maxxum, a camera driven by two eight-bit microprocessors that is, along with the Canon T80, our nomination for the best of the new generation of automatic 35-mm SLRs.

But most 35-mm SLRs are the semiautomatics, and these are still the preferred cameras among the pros and the more demanding amateurs. There's no doubt they take more savvy to operate, but that's because they're packed with options. Take the Nikon F3A4 for a starter. With Nikkor lenses it can focus automatically—or, if you'd prefer, it'll just give its opinion as to how it thinks it should be focused. A mirror-chamber diode continuously monitors light, weighting its measurement toward the center where, presumably, your subject may be found. It also measures light reflected from the film, for auto exposure flash.

This is generally considered to be a camera for professionals and, according to *Modern Photography*, the auto-focus is as precise as a pro's eye. As you might expect, this machine is the basic component of a system that is adaptable to motor drive, bulk packs, and a variety of viewfinders.

Right up there with the Nikon F3A4 are Canon's New F-1 and the Olympus OM-4. The New F-1 gets high marks for its rugged body, versatile metering system, and wide range of shutter speeds. The OM-4 is highly regarded for the precision of its multiple metering modes. One very interesting feature is its ability to bracket exposure automatically by averaging the readings of as many as eight different objects in your composition.

Our choice for second best is an updated version of one of the most popular semiautomatics of all time. The Canon AE-1 Program is designed to do everything the AE-1 could do, and more. It happily combines the latest in electronic technology with all the traditional, manually operated features that are dear to the hearts of true shutterbugs.

The AE-1's fully automatic exposure control is operated by a silicon photodiode metering circuit that sets both shutter speed and aperture in the auto mode or just gives good advice in the manual setting. The new LED readouts are an enormous improvement over the old needle indicator, and the split-image rangefinder no longer dims half the image at wide f-stops. Shutter speeds range from two seconds to one one-thousandth of a second, along with B and an X sync of one-sixtieth of a second. A red *P* will flash on in the viewfinder when the shutter speed falls below the slowest safe hand-held speed of one-thirtieth of a second. Likewise, f-stop indicators blink when there is a threat of over- or underexposure at the minimum and maximum ends of the aperture range. Best of all, the AE-1 can be found for as little as half the price of the cameras listed above.

Just keep in mind that the camera is a deceptive tool. As photo critic Beaumont Newhall says in an introduction to a recent collection of the works of photographer Arnold Newman, "With today's technology mediocre results can be achieved automatically. Unfortunately, mediocrity is all too often confused with success; we are too easily pleased."

Time to Buy a Car

*"Christmas Eve, and twelve
  of the clock.
Now they are all on their
  knees . . ."*

THE best time to buy a new car is when you don't want one—really, it makes sense. Even those without a taste for paradox will recognize that the auto industry gives nothing away for nothing. It knows what you want and what you'll pay for it. And inevitably, you do. In consequence, the only chance you have of turning things to your advantage is by acting atypically—and this, we hardly need add, is something few of us can achieve.

So make the most of it, all you oddballs, fringe-dwellers, denizens of statistical abnormality, for once the cards are actually stacked in your favor. Multiply your squints, tics, and impenetrable motivations, and get along down to the showrooms, where (boy!) have they got a deal for you. Want a Yugoslavian convertible in January? You'll make out like a bandit. One of those Detroit Destructo family wagons, facing recall and outlawed by three consumer associations? Hey, we're talking rebates and the ranch-style body molding thrown in for free. For it's a melancholy fact that the further we depart from the norms. of predictable (and sensible) behavior, the better chance we have of extracting concessions in the form of low interest rates, price reductions, and add-on options at no extra fee.

But what about the rest of us, those with no obvious death-wish, who have at least heard of *Consumer Reports?* Well, it's generally understood you can get a better deal on a new car at the end of the model year. After all, most new car buyers want something that's *new*. From August onward, these status seekers will wait a couple of months to get the next year's styling, and knowing this, by November dealers usually take a cut in profit on the older models or throw in some options at no cost.

But for buyers, this enticement is full of contradiction, since in order to make it work you've got to have a consumer habit that's atypical to a highly atypical degree. If you make a trade-in after twenty-five months, which is roughly the national average, you'll find the car assessed as a three-year-old in the Blue Book. So in terms of financial advantage, you'll have done yourself no good at all. And besides, there's another factor: manufacturers nowadays put their prices up at capricious intervals, and in the case of imported vehicles, probably several times throughout the model year. The end result of this is that even if you *do* make a killing in November, the vehicle will probably still cost you more than you would have paid eight months before.

Of course, you can wait for rebates and—a popular enticement in the last couple of years—manufacturers' low-interest loans. But essentially, the principle's the same: you're being paid to be weird. Unpopular models, unattractively large down payments, and prohibitively short payback periods are really what's on sale. On top of that, you'll almost certainly be buying from dealer stock, which will probably mean taking a host of unsalable options whose cost the dealer will inevitably try to recover. So when you're looking at that candy pink Escort with smoked windows and the spoiler, it might be a good idea to bear in mind the resale value. Last, many factory incentives require dealer participation. This means that the dealer is expected either to take a cut in profit or to "buy" part of your lower interest rate. So if you plan to storm the showrooms with that look you practiced in assertiveness training, don't waste the calories. The dealers are not going to come down any lower than their usual minimum, plus whatever they need to make up the lost revenue.

However, dealerships have problems of their own. Like most organizations, they have to reconcile the unyielding principles by which they operate with the inevitable fluctuations of human behavior. Overhead, (in the form of advertising and promotional costs), ground rent, and all the steady expenses of keeping a business running present themselves with calendrical regularity. On top of this, managers are usually locked in an endless series of sales projections, resulting in not just monthly, but weekly, daily, and even hourly quotas. They can't relax until they see the customers' names go up on the sales board each day. If the showroom is still empty by noontime, they start to sweat. If there's a thunderstorm all afternoon keeping buyers at home, then by evening they're ready to start talking. And if this happens to be at the end of a bad month generally, you'll be amazed at the concessions they'll make to get your business. Come in the next week on a sunny morning, and you'll find a whole different picture.

So which are the bad times for dealers? Or, to ask the same question differently, which are the *good* times for buyers? Well, first there are the traditional seasons when ordinary buyer activity is low. At Christmas and around New Year's, for instance, when consumers are dipping into their pockets for other expenses, obviously, down payments are hard to scrape together, and in consequence car sales slump. Also, look out for highly publicized sale weeks; for while these don't always mean a dealership's hard up for business, they do mean additional advertising and promotional costs to recover. And whenever there's an upset in the usual customer/cost ratio, the salesperson's always under greater pressure to make a deal. Finally, there are slumps in demand that are peculiar to the automobile industry and are apparently unrelated to the general business cycle. Next to home ownership, buying a car is by far the heaviest financial commitment the average consumer makes, and as such, subject to complex tides of caution and opportunity imperceptible to consumers generally. Inexplicably, car sales might be depressed for several weeks or months, a trend made obvious only by reports in the business press and perhaps a flurry of extravagant advertising by dealers. Although the chances are that you too will be subject to the same influences, these are the weeks to buy.

So the odds aren't all against you. But, as we have seen, what consumer advantage mostly boils down to is being different—either in choice of purchase or in buying habits, and this is something most of us just don't want to be. So while unquestionably the best time to buy a car is when no one else in the universe will touch the model, when it's stacking up on dealer lots and dogs howl at its shadow, the second best time is probably on a rainy Sunday evening at the end of December. But don't forget, this is only when the dealer is *most likely to bargain*. You've still got to get the price down yourself.

Umbrella

Swingin' in the rain

THE best umbrellas in the world are sold by James Smith & Sons at 53 Oxford Street, London WC1. The Smith family has been in the umbrella and walking stick game since 1830. They haven't changed their working methods since Victoria was on the throne and Lord Palmerston was living at 10 Downing Street; and they will repair any umbrella they have ever sold.

In this category, best and second best are variations on the classic twenty-five-inch 'brolly, which is required outerwear in the vicinity of Whitehall and the City. (Bowlers are now optional, if not downright recherché). If their *best* is the traditional Malacca cane-handled umbrella (the cane fitted over beech or some other stronger wood, with a flat black nylon cover), *second* best is simply the same model with the Malacca cane fitted over a metal tube, cutting the £60-plus price roughly in half.

Telescoping umbrellas are convenient, but are an abomination to the traditionalist, and you'll not be wanting a paisley or plaid cover if you intend to dress for success in the City. Solid-handled umbrellas include chestnut, hickory, and ash—all well suited to country use. Rhinoceros-horn handles are also available for $500, but we wouldn't recommend that you carry this model to fund-raisers for the International Wildlife Fund. Gold- or silver-plated monogrammed lap bands are a permissible ostentation.

Weight Machine (Personal)

Home bodies

WE'RE going to keep this discussion of weight machines short but sweet. Let's face it, weight machines are *not* sex or politics or baseball. It's a subject that can be beaten to death in almost no time.

You're looking at weight machines for your home. The first thing you want is a *multi-station* weight machine, i.e., one that will let you do a number of different exercises on one unit. You look around for the best one, and you see that it's something like the Ariel 4000. This beauty was designed by Israel's Dr. Gideon Ariel, who uses it to train Olympic athletes at his California training center. It has a computer. It has program discs. It gives you real-time readouts on how you're doing, measured against how you *were* doing in the past. You can hook up the display terminal so you can watch soap operas. If you find yourself in possession of some inside information, you can even punch up stock quotations. And how much does this beauty cost? About $17,000.

You conclude that maybe you don't deserve the best. What are the criteria for picking out the best of the rest? J. Patrick Netter, author of *High-Tech Fitness* and proprietor of Hollywood's High-Tech Fitness retail outlet, sells such devices and knows all about them. Here's what he recommends you look for:

1. The frame of your machine should be strong enough to bear its load of weight—as well as the weight of your body.
2. Welded construction is better than bolts. Bolts can work loose if you bang them around, and you're going to be banging your weight machine around every time you use it.
3. Welds should be smooth and clean.
4. Pulleys and cables should be strong and should operate smoothly. Any part of the lifting mechanism that's even slightly jerky or wobbly on the showroom floor will get much worse over time. And we're not talking about much time, either.
5. You shouldn't have to be a German car mechanic to knock down the unit, or to change its configuration to do various exercises.
6. It should adjust to fit *you* comfortably. Most exercise devices, like most everything else, are designed for people of roughly average size.
7. Weight standards (those upright things that actually support the barbell) or handles should be spaced wide enough apart to be comfortable.
8. The paint shouldn't come off on the floor.
9. The manufacturer should be an established one. That means he'll

be around for awhile, and his service agent will be able to help you if you have a problem.

10. The bench should be well padded and comfortable. We've put this last, but in any order of importance, it's very close to first.

What multi-station weight unit meets these criteria? The Paramount Fitnessmate. Paramount is an old name in the gym equipment biz, and this machine features a chest and shoulder press bar, a high pulley for pull-downs, a low pulley for rowing, an adjustable incline bench, rollers for leg curls and extensions, and an optional pec deck. Its action is unusually smooth. At $1,500–$2,200 (depending on attachments, custom upholstery, and whether or not you want the weight plates chrome-plated), the Fitnessmate is an exceptional value for the money.

Wines
That Are
neither Red
nor White

We blush to drink

REMEMBER when wines came in just three colors? There were red and white and, in between, rosé. But somehow, with the rise of the neither-red-nor-white as the official drink of the Y-generation, these careful distinctions were lost. Now the middle ground has expanded to include a spectrum of new wines in search of a market and a catchy descriptive label. The new hues include blush (a registered trademark of Mill Creek Winery); blanc de noir; pink; oeil de perdrix (meaning "eye of the partridge," but difficulty with its pronunciation and uncertainty as to the exact hue of partridge eyes doesn't make this a popular term); and, most confusing of all, white (even though it clearly is not).

White zinfandels (just say "white zin") are the most popular of the neither-nors. The top scorer in national wine tastings is DeLoach Vineyards' zin; but in recent tastings in California, Bel Arbres' vivid pink zin has come in as a strong contender, and though it has yet to prove itself in a wider market, it's our choice for second best. It is rich, spicy, and not so sweet that it can't be served as a dinner wine.

Of the pinot noir blancs, Paloma Vineyards' Blanc de Noir and Buena Vista's Blanc de Pinot Noir are consistently ranked at the top by oenophiles and the editors of wine industry magazines, who seem to spend a lot of time traveling around the world drinking wine (we're inclined to consider a career change). But for second best we recommend Stony Ridge's Pinot Noir Blanc. Like Bel Arbres' zin, it is doing well in tastings and, perhaps more significantly, in the marketplace as well. It's spicy, with a slight cherry bouquet, and is a trifle on the sweet side, but it's almost always available at bargain prices.

Proprietary blanc de noirs and blush brands have the most interesting names (*Sunset Cuvée* and *Alpenglow*), but they are not among our favorite neither-nors. If we must, we'll have a glass of Pedroncelli's Sonoma Blush (Mr. Pedroncelli must pay Mill Creek a little less than a penny a bottle to use the term *blush*). And for second best, we'll go for Nevada City Winery's Alpenglow because we like its spritzy, strawberry taste and because we like the name.

Among the white cabernets, Sterling Vineyards Cabernet Blanc has been consistently ranked at or near the top in recent tastings; but when we compared it to a few less well-distributed wines that had not gone up against Sterling, our tasters agreed that Fallbrook Vineyards' Olive Hill Tourmaline Blanc is not only an excellent choice for second best, it's an even better value for the money. It has a startlingly intense pink color with a wonderful, creamy texture, good body, and a restrained cabernet taste.

There are a wide range of varietal rosés, but Worden's Washington Gamay is a reliable bet, generally regarded as one of the best. Our favorite, and our choice for second best, is Cresta Blanca's Mendocino Gamay Rose, which has a tart cherry aroma but tastes slightly of cranberries (by all means, serve it with the turkey). And it is generally priced so low as to arouse suspicion—but this may not be a lasting phenomenon.

Pure
Silver

Witticism by Oscar Wilde

Nothing to declare

In an idle hour, we once picked up a book with the promising title *Lives of the Wits* by Hesketh Pearson. After several hundred pages, we reached two conclusions. The first was that there are a limited number of witty things to say, and so they tend to get reinvented. For example: when Henry Labouchère, the nineteenth-century parliamentarian, was a young secretary at the British legation in St. Petersburg, a "self-important noble-man" came to call on the ambassa-dor. " 'Pray take a chair; he will be here soon,' said Labby. 'But, young man, do you know who I am?' and the visitor recited his distinctions. 'Pray take two chairs,' said Labby." This is (almost) exactly what Dick

Cavett said to Norman Mailer the night Mailer announced that he was much smarter than Cavett, Gore Vidal, and writer Janet Flanner (who happened to be Cavett's other guests on his television talk show) put together. Cavett vacated his chair and when Mailer asked why, said: "So your giant intellect can sit down."

Our second conclusion was that spontaneous wit does not age well. (Was Jonathan Swift *really* being funny when he greeted a friend's wife with "Pox on you, you slut!"? Maybe you had to be there.) Oscar Wilde, playwright and aesthete, is the great exception—still fresh, funny, and confounding to conventional wisdom after all these years. (He died in 1900 in Paris, in a shabby furnished room, whose cabbage-rose wallpaper he abhorred. According to legend, his last words were: "Either that wallpaper goes, or I do.")

At Oxford, Wilde graduated with a rare "double first." For his examination in Greek he did a sight translation from the New Testament. "The passage chosen was from the story of the Passion. Wilde began to translate, easily and accurately. The examiners were satisfied, and told him that this was enough. Wilde ignored them and continued to translate. After another attempt the examiners at last succeeded in stopping him, and told him that they were satisfied with his translation. 'Oh, do let me go on,' said Wilde, 'I want to see how it ends.' "

Wilde was (reasonably enough) suspected of rehearsing beforehand the sayings he tossed off at London dinner parties, such as "Work is the curse of the drinking classes" and "The woman who hesitates is won." ("Familiarity breeds consent" is another line in a similar vein.)

But second best was his spontaneous reply to the customs official who asked, "Have you anything to declare?" when he arrived in New York in 1882.

"No. I have nothing to declare," he replied, and then he paused. "Except my genius."

Zen Master

Mu!

Our favorite, though we do not nominate him as best or second best, was Ma-tsu, a Chinese master of the eighth century. According to the chronicles, "His appearance was remarkable. He strode along like a bull and glared about him like a tiger. If he stretched out his tongue, it reached over his nose; on the soles of his feet were imprinted two circular marks." Once he assisted a disciple in gaining enlightenment by twisting his nose.

By its own reckoning, Zen is very ancient. Bodhidharma, the semi-legendary founder of Zen in China (or Ch'an in Mandarin), sailed for Cathay from India in the middle of the sixth century, and according to tradition, he was the twenty-eighth Indian patriarch.

Bodhidharma's career in China has an air of the absurd that is (how to put it?) positively Zennish. Arriving in China, he was summoned to Nanking for an audience with the Emperor Wu, known to be a devout Buddhist. "I have built many temples and monasteries," said the emperor. "I have copied the sacred books of the Buddha. Now what is my merit?"

"None whatever, your Majesty!" Bodhidharma cheerfully replied.

Trying a new tack, the emperor asked, "What is to be considered the First Principle of the Dharma?"

"Vast Emptiness, and nothing holy therein," Bodhidharma replied.

Emperor Wu: "Who then confronts me?"

Bodhidharma: "I have no idea."

Afterward, Bodhidharma retired to a monastery on Mount Sung, where he sat gazing at a wall for nine years, until his legs withered away. According to another tradition, he was seen after his death, passing through the Western Gates of China with a sandal on his head.

Most Zen *koans* (anecdotes or paradoxes of the masters, set as problems for disciples) date from the T'ang dynasty in China, during the "Golden Age of Zen" (A.D. 713–845). As in, "A monk once asked, 'What is Buddha?' The master replied, 'Three pounds of flax.'" Or, yet more obscurely, from Huang-lung's "Three Barriers":

QUESTION: In what way do my feet resemble the feet of a donkey?
ANSWER: When the heron stands in the snow, its color is not the same.

Which might be a poem by Wallace Stevens.

Chu-chih, another master of this period, practiced "One-Finger Zen." Following the example of *his* master, T-ien-lung, he simply raised one finger in answer to any question put to him. Inevitably, the day came when one of his disciples answered a question with the same gesture. Hearing about this, Chu-chih descended on him like the wrath of God and cut off the disciple's offending finger. Howling with pain, the novice started to run off, whereupon Chu-chih called him back, and, having got his full attention, raised one finger—whereupon, the annals record, "the disciple attained enlightenment."

For most of the last thousand years, Zen has been primarily a Japanese phenomenon, and the greatest figure in Japanese Zen Buddhism—hence, for our purposes, the "best" historical Zen master—is Dogen-Zenji (1200–1253), who founded the Soto school. He was an extreme ascetic, possessed by a sense of the transitoriness of things. "In the morning rosy cheeks, in the evening a pale skeleton."

According to historian Heinrich Dumoulin, "next to Dogen" was Hakuin (1685–1768), painter, memoirist of genius, and reformer of the noisy and antic Rinzai school. Like Dogon, Hakuin was haunted early on by transience. The sight of clouds changing over the sea is said to have made him weep as a child.

Hakuin was driven half out of his mind trying to solve the *koan*, "Does a dog have Buddha nature?" Happily, though, he succeeded and in his old age devised the most famous *koan* of all, "What is the sound of one hand clapping?" He was kindly to the poor and downtrodden, which was certainly not the case with many aristocratic Zen masters, and was a great popularizer. In a remarkable self-portrait, he looks rather gloomy, but then in the preface to his "Chat on a Boat in the Evening," he signs himself "The hungry and frozen one burning incense and bowing down his head."

Incidentally, our consultant the Buddhologist initially declined our request that he name the best and second best *koans*, saying you can't hierarchize these things; that's missing the point, etc.; but finally conceded that well, the one *koan* profounder than Hakuin's was the one by the Chinese master Chao-chou that Hakuin was brooding about.

QUESTION: What is the Buddha-nature of a dog?
ANSWER: Wu!

Or in Japanese, "Mu!" Meaning, emptiness.

Well, he's the Buddhologist, but *we* still like the one about the Buddha being three pounds of flax.

Zoo

Wild classroom

THE first modern zoo is still the most architecturally elegant. Vienna's Schoenbrunn was built in 1752 by the emperor Francis I as a gift for his wife, Maria Theresa, who liked pets. What they did in the privacy of their baroque pavilion at the center of the exhibits, which radiate outward like spokes of an enormous wheel, is a question history leaves unanswered. But the imperial couple would hardly recognize many of today's cageless zoos, built on the principles of zoogeographic, participatory landscape design by boards of directors eager to compete for the family fun dollar with the vast new pleasure domes of Walt Disney and his spiritual heirs.

The best are Miami's Metro Zoo, where Bengal tigers relax on the grounds of their very own Cambodian Buddhist temple ruin; San Diego's Zoo and Wild Animal Park that offer a complete Nairobi village and a monorail ride over an animal-packed landscape that Isak Dinesen would feel at home in; the Woodland Park Zoo in Seattle, which, despite the rainy climate, has managed to build a replica of the Sonoran desert, in addition to a Patagonian pond and an African savanna; the London Zoo, because it's in London; and the Singapore Zoological Gardens, fantastically lush, set on a series of islands surrounded by the vast Seletar Reservoir, easily the most beautiful zoo in the world.

But our choice for second best was founded just twenty-five years ago by naturalist Gerald Durrell. It may not have the range and quantity of animals found in more traditional zoos, and facilities for visitors are Spartan by comparison. For these reasons you will never find it listed among the best, at least not until the animals themselves get to cast their votes. Bathed by the warm waters and invigorating breezes of the Gulf Stream, the equable climate of the island of Jersey in the English Channel seemed to Durrell an ideal site for a zoo. But it's not the un-British climate, or the natural beauty of the countryside, or the charm of the nearby villages, that earns the Jersey Zoo our respect. It is the dedication of Durrell and his colleagues to the salvation and preservation of some of the world's most endangered species.

The Jersey Zoo's breeding successes include such rare species as the spectacled bear, the lowland gorilla and the pink pigeon. But the staff's proudest achievement is the creation of an international training center dedicated to teaching the techniques of wildlife preservation to students from around the world. These programs are evidence that this zoo, at least, is still more interested in its animals than its visitors. Well worth a visit.